MW01194131

The
YES
ANXIETY

Taming the Fear
of Commitment in

- ❏ *Relationships*
- ❏ Career
- ❏ *Spiritual Life*
- ❏ Daily Decisions

M. Blaine Smith

SilverCrest
B•O•O•K•S

SilverCrest Books
P.O. Box 448
Damascus, Maryland 20872

e-mail: scr@nehemiahministries.com
www.nehemiahministries.com

ISBN: 978-0-9840322-1-1

Contents

PART ONE

Confronting the Fear of Commitment

CHAPTER ONE

A Peril to Growth, a Bombshell in Relationships

It's a Saturday afternoon and a woman from Houston phones me. I met Carla briefly on a singles retreat I led several months ago. In one of my talks that weekend I spoke briefly of the fear of commitment and noted that many Christians today struggle with it. Her interest was piqued. She hopes now to talk with me more than briefly about her own fears, which threaten to derail her engagement.

"I've dated this wonderful man for more than two years and have longed to marry him," she explains. "But since accepting Allen's proposal two weeks ago, I've barely slept and haven't been able to take in much food. My whole system has shut down. I'm so frightened I'm nearly paralyzed."

I ask for some detail about her background. I find that Carla comes from a caring, supportive family and has long been active in strong evangelical churches. At twenty-seven, she holds a challenging job teaching third grade in a public school. After chatting with her a few minutes, I'm convinced she is a mature, compassionate Christian dealing with more than self-centered issues. At different points I press her to tell me if she has any reservations about marrying Allen. Her fears may be signaling something critical—that underneath she doubts he would be a good husband. But not once during our two-hour conversation can she pinpoint a single problem with Allen or their relationship. Instead, she describes his many strong points and does a good job convincing me he would be an ideal partner for her.

Still, she is plagued with fears that dumbfound her. I ask about her experience with other major decisions—have they been as painful to make as this one? She admits they have all been traumatic. Choosing a college and a major, leaving home, deciding where to work, finding a place to live—these all have been gut-wrenching steps. Making a binding decision simply goes against her nature.

Finally, we get to the heart of her problem. More than any specific doubt, it's the fear of being penned in that holds her back. To the extent that a major change is binding, she feels as jumpy as a cornered animal. Since marriage, more than any other step, means no turning back, it brings out her worst fears of being trapped.

In short, Carla fears commitment itself. To say she is phobic about commitment is not to state it too strongly. The implications are tragic in her case for, without relief from her panic, she'll break her engagement to Allen.

Carla's predicament is not in any way unusual, nor is her example extreme. I counsel with many who, like her, are excessively fearful of commitment. While their decision areas vary greatly, their apprehensions are similar. Often they feel torn between extremes— longing to take a step forward yet dreading the thought of being locked in.

Many break the mold of the person we would expect to resist commitment. Far from being lethargic or irresponsible, they are bright, talented, energetic and spiritually competent. Many are outgoing individuals, not at all shy and generally confident. Yet they acutely fear trusting their own judgment and being drawn into any obligation that is binding. And like a chronic disease or disability, their fear forces a wedge between what they would like to do and what they feel capable of accomplishing.

When We Fear What We Really Want

When we look honestly at what we most want from life, we find that most of us hold several ambitions in common.

We long for our life to accomplish something significant. We want to know that what we do has lasting benefit to others and that our example is influencing others in positive ways.

We earnestly desire to be loved for who we are. We thirst for deep relationships. We particularly crave the incomparable benefits of long-term acquaintances.

And we want to grow. We discover over time that our greatest joy comes from being in a growth mode. We long to develop our potential, to be creative, to experience the stimulation of new adventures.

It might be added that we yearn for security, which in its most wholesome sense means having enough stability and comfort in life to pursue these other goals.

These are worthy aspirations. They are part of the life instinct God has put within us, central to having a healthy will to live. Our fulfillment and our fruitfulness depend heavily upon pursuing these goals and pursuing them passionately.

Yet not one of them can be realized without extreme patience, enduring dedication and sacrifice—in short, *commitment.* There's the rub: While we relish the benefits of commitment, we dislike its requirements. It always means giving up certain freedoms and taking on new obligations.

Many factors at the end of the twentieth century dampen our zeal for commitment—especially for making those commitments that are needed to realize our fullest potential for Christ. The unspeakable materialism of modern life easily lulls us into complacency. The constant idealizing of situations in human life by the media causes us to despise the real-life opportunities we have. The unprecedented freedom of choice we enjoy works against us as well. Not only is it dizzying to weigh the options in any decision. It is frustrating to let go of the luxury of having all these wonderful options before us. It is too easy to become *addicted to the freedom of not committing ourselves.*

So most of us, at this time in history, feel hesitant to commit—even to good opportunities for realizing our potential. But some people, like Carla, face a much more serious challenge. Beyond the normal hesitations we all experience, they have an ingrained fear of commitment. They dread being drawn into any situation where they will feel locked in. Their fear of losing freedom is so extreme that they may even sabotage their own effort to reach important goals. When resistance to commitment is this strong, it is more than a matter of simple laziness: it results from deep, complex factors. Yet the problem is usually not well understood by those who haven't experienced it.

It's often not well understood even by those who *do* experience it! Commitment-fearful people often imagine they are more capable of forging commitments than they are. They may even enter them confidently. Yet soon second thoughts strike with a vengeance. They are consumed with regret over what they are leaving behind and with fear over the new obligations ahead. At this point they often stun others and sometimes themselves by reneging on the pledges they have made.

Of course, many who fear commitment simply balk at making any commitments at all. In either case, commitment-fearful people too often fail to realize their potential and to accomplish goals they dearly want to reach.

A Puzzling Predicament

While I've long realized that some people fear commitment, only in recent years have I recognized how serious the problem can be.

Counseling singles considering marriage, more than any other factor, has helped me appreciate just how severely some people fear commitment. In the late 1980s I began offering a seminar on choosing a marriage partner. Then I published *Should I Get Married?* on the same subject. From this new focus in my teaching came greater opportunity to interact with Christians who are trying to resolve the direction of a relationship.

The response to *Should I Get Married?* was a real surprise. When I wrote that book, I tacked on a short section at the end—almost as an afterthought—on the fear of commitment. Since its publication, most of my contacts from readers have been in regard to that one section: they want to talk with me about their own struggles with commitment.

Most of the stories are similar. They've been in a strong, long-term relationship with someone they dearly want to marry. But now it has reached the commitment stage and they're panicked. They may be experiencing physical distress. Some are obsessed with imperfections in their partner which haven't been issues before. Others, like Carla, cannot give any clear reason at all for their fear. Many confess to being puzzled at their panic and uncertain how it fits with their belief that God gives perfect peace to those he leads into marriage. Some are afraid to admit their anxieties to anyone, fearing they will be judged unspiritual or out of God's will.

Brad, a twenty-nine-year-old teacher in a Christian college, drove two hours to speak with me. He explained that he had been dating Kelly for nearly two years and often felt convinced they should marry. Friends and family agreed they were an ideal match. Every time Brad and Kelly talked seriously about marriage, he felt "on the mountaintop" for a day or two. But then panic set in—so intense that he was disoriented for several days. "I feel as though there is a giant bubble in my chest, pressing against my heart, as though I'm about to have a heart attack," he confessed. Only by admitting to Kelly that he needed more time did he find any relief.

Mitch, a thirty-year-old pastor in a small midwestern city, phoned me just six weeks before his wedding. He explained that he was engaged to an extraordinary woman he had known for many years and he was certain she would make an excellent wife. "But whenever I even think about going through with marriage, I experience a pain in my stomach so piercing I can't eat," he complained. "I'm consumed with anxiety about taking this step." He wondered if God was warning him through his fear not to go ahead. He added that there was no one in his church or community with whom he could unload. Folks in his town wouldn't think it proper for a pastor to experience such fears.

Susan, a thirty-four-year-old computer specialist in Newport, Rhode Island, had meticulously weighed her decision to marry Herb over the course of a four-year relationship. She knew he would be a supportive husband, strong spiritual leader and excellent provider. And she loved him deeply. She recognized, too, that her prospects for finding another opportunity at her age were not good. Besides, few men would be willing to put up with her erratic mood swings. Still, in several long conversations this bright, seasoned Christian explained that Herb fell short of her ideals in certain ways. Susan wondered if she could find someone more suitable by waiting longer. Each time she resolved these issues, they resurfaced a week or two later. She spoke, too, of being desperately afraid of going into marriage. She phoned me just one week before her wedding, so panic-stricken she was ready to call it off.

I could fill this book with similar stories. Of course, not everyone who fears committing to marriage dreads it this intensely. And fear sometimes indicates one has legitimate concerns which need to be examined. Still, in many cases the hesitation to marry springs from an underlying anxiety about commitment itself. Commitment fear clouds the thinking of many who are considering marriage—and prompts some to turn their back on golden opportunities.

Don't Fence Me In
Christians fear commitment in other areas too. Many who fear com-

mitting to marriage tell me that they fear committing in other decision areas as well. Their experiences have deepened my awareness of the difficulties Christians—married and single—face with commitment at many points in life. While romantic relationships provide some of the most dramatic examples, "the yes anxiety" hinders people in many other ways.

Marriage and family life. Some people survive the dating and engagement stage fine but then panic once married. Now they feel claustrophobic, like someone trapped in an elevator. This fallout may occur early in a marriage, after the birth of a child or at some later turning point or crisis.

Career. The fear of being penned in also plagues many in their career and professional life. Some find the prospect of success itself unsettling. They may bounce from job to job or settle for employment well beneath their potential. Not a few sabotage their own efforts at success, bailing out of a job unnecessarily or behaving in a manner that gets them fired.

Church and ministry commitments. Christians often display strong avoidance patterns in their commitment to church and spiritual growth. They may long to grow spiritually and to have a personal ministry. Yet they find it hard to stick with any activity long enough to reap the benefits. They join a Bible study or agree to teach a Sunday-school class, then quit a few weeks later when the experience no longer seems fresh. They change churches frequently or drop out altogether. In the campus setting, students hop from Christian group to group and balk at assuming responsibility.

Other areas. The commitment-fearful person often has considerable difficulty sticking with personal disciplines and resolutions. Whether it's a devotional time, an exercise routine, a dietary regimen, a moral pledge, a promise about savings or a decision to develop a talent, the priority gets quickly shelved.

Resolving *any* decision can be painful for this person. She vacillates in choosing where to live, breaking promises to several roommates along the way. She decides to rent rather than buy, so she'll be less obligated if she wants to move. The "buyer's remorse" reaction is also common. He tries on three dozen sports coats, finally finds one he likes and buys it. The next day he returns it, convinced he's made the mistake of his life.

In many other ways the commitment-fearful person hedges at being obligated. If you've tried to pin her down on weekend or vacation plans, you know what I mean. His ongoing concern can be stated simply: Keep the options open.

Commitment fear holds many back from doing what is in their best interest. Even when they find the resolve to go ahead, they still suffer much unnecessary distress. And valuable time and energy is wasted fretting over second thoughts and coming to terms with mood swings.

Steps Toward Healing
For some time I've been troubled by the moralistic emphasis on commitment in so much Christian preaching, teaching, writing and sometimes even counseling. So often the message is, "Recognize your obligation to God. Stop evading responsibility. Commit yourself, even if it hurts." Unfortunately this message, which appeals more to guilt than to positive motivation, only aggravates the problem for commitment-fearful Christians, who already feel guilty enough for their failings. They are well aware they need to make commitments, be resolute and take greater initiative with their life. They know all about the demands of Christian duty. Yet fears and instincts too often get the upper hand and hold them back.

If you chronically fear commitment, you are not likely to reach the point of committing confidently without going through a significant personal transformation. For most, this involves four critical steps.

1. You need to understand clearly what frightens you about commitment and why. You need your issues and concerns carefully addressed. In the areas where commitment frightens you, you need to learn to reshape your outlook to more accurately reflect how God

sees the Christian life.

2. You need to learn how to respond to mood swings and manage runaway emotions. Chronic commitment fear is always as much an instinctive reaction as it is a problem of perspective. Commitment-fearful people often suffer extreme emotional swings and vacillating impressions about God's will. You need to understand how to reduce your vulnerability to mood shifts and to recognize God's will amid your maze of feelings. You also need to learn how to respond effectively to the emotion of fear itself. Commitment fear often reaches the level of a phobia, taking on a life of its own. Understanding practical ways to break the panic cycle can make a radical difference.

3. You need a fuller understanding of the benefits of commitment and a stronger desire for them. While most commitment-fearful people recognize that commitment is important, their understanding of *how* it will benefit them is limited. They are more conscious of what they will lose by committing themselves than of what they will gain. Gaining a greater appreciation for the benefits of commitment will strengthen your motivation both to confront your fear and to take steps of faith in spite of it.

4. Finally, commitment-fearful people need moral encouragement to take the steps which frighten them. The time comes when it's important to make commitments even though some fears and doubts remain. You need help in knowing how to recognize this point and encouragement to move ahead. You need to be convinced you can handle any experience of fear involved and come through it unscathed. You need assurance that you are capable of sticking with the commitments you make. And you need stronger confidence that God desires the best for you, is giving you the grace to make wise choices and is protecting you as you move forward.

My hope in this book is to give as much help as possible along these lines to commitment-fearful people. In the four sections which follow, I want to look closely at each of these areas of need and offer the best insight and counsel that I can. I write this book with two strong convictions about emotional healing. One is that the healing of deep-seated conflicts is always a process. It takes time, persistence and dedicated effort. At the same time, significant progress can be made at each stage of this effort. Scripture shows consistently that God is on our side as we confront our emotional struggles. Once we open ourselves to his help, he gives us success at many surprising points. From the moment I decide to take determined steps toward healing, I move from a position of defeat to one of victory in dealing with my problem.

For this reason, my approach in this book is consistently practical. With each topic my purpose is not merely to analyze the problem but to suggest changes in outlook and practical steps you can take to move beyond your inhibitions. This book is dedicated not merely to examining the problem of commitment fear but to helping readers find healing, a process which can begin with the next chapter.

My primary concern is to help Christians who suffer from chronic commitment anxiety. Yet I also want to give encouragement to those whose struggles are less serious. Perhaps you are less than comfortable with commitment. Certain inclinations make it hard for you to settle decisions—a perfectionist mentality, for instance, or a tendency toward strong mood swings. Yet commitment doesn't frighten you to the point of sweaty palms, palpitations and the sensation of air bubbles pressing against your heart. You are generally able to resolve your choices and move on. Still you would like help in becoming more resolute and confident about the commitments you make.

Your situation is much in my mind throughout this book. You should find plenty of practical material that addresses your needs. You may find, too, that some of the book's topics relate more clearly to your needs than others. Feel free to begin at any point in the book and read just those portions that most obviously help you. The book is designed so you can do that. Different topics will be the primary areas of struggle for different readers.

One further point about the book's contents. Beyond the dread of being penned in and losing freedom which troubles all who fear commitment, there are three distinct concerns which many commitment-anxious people experience: the fear of *making an imperfect decision,* the fear of *success* and the fear of *losing ownership of their life.* While some commitment-fearful people experience all of these anxieties, many experience only one or two. Any of them is sufficient to trigger serious commitment-fear reactions. I will examine each of these concerns in detail.

Staying Hopeful
While I've known many Christians who have struggled with commitment fear, it has been a joy to see many overcome their inhibitions and find the courage to take the steps which once seemed impossible for them. Carla, for instance, is now happily married and eternally grateful she didn't let her apprehensions hold her back. Examples like hers inspire me to write and convince me that anyone who makes the effort can experience significant healing and substantial victory over commitment fear. It's with that hope that I offer these reflections. May God apply the truth where needed in your own life, and may your commitment to read this book be rewarded in many ways.

CHAPTER TWO

Seeing the Best When It's Less Than Perfect

We face two ongoing challenges in all of the decisions we make. One is to see the flaws in opportunities which at first seem only too perfect.

A friend tells me that he once had the chance to marry a woman whom he worshiped. "I thank God now that it didn't work out," he says, "because I would have ceased to be who I am."

My friend showed uncanny wisdom in turning away from this enchanting option. Although he was greatly attracted to this woman, he concluded that marrying her wouldn't be right in light of how God had made him as a person. It would have diverted his attention from areas where he needed to grow, and important areas of his potential would never have been realized.

It's often this way with opportunities which are too enticing. The most alluring prospects in relationships, jobs and other areas can have a way of consuming us. We become so obsessed with our absorbing interest that we stop enjoying other areas of life as fully, and our growth is stunted. Ironically, it's those opportunities which most perfectly match our dreams and fantasies that often pose the greatest danger, for we're least likely to consider the tradeoffs involved in pursuing them. Learning to think clearly in the face of such choices is no small challenge.

But seeing the imperfections in "perfect" opportunities is only half the battle in making healthy decisions. We also need to be able to recognize the value of opportunities that we're inclined to turn down because they seem to fall short of our ideals. God often has remarkable opportunities for us that we tend to undervalue. We see them as good opportunities but not perfect ones. Yet God sees them as the *right* opportunities for us, given the total mix of factors in our life.

Appreciating these openings for what they are is a particularly difficult challenge for the commitment-fearful person. A major part of what fuels commitment fear is the dread of compromising or "settling." Most people who fear commitment are inordinately concerned about being drawn into situations that do not perfectly meet their ideals. Their sensibilities are finely tuned to imperfections in people, relationships, work situations—all the opportunities life offers. They are slow to commit to opportunities others would find welcome and quick to bail out of situations that fail to live up to their standards.

Accepting that God's best for us can seem less than perfect is a major step in taming this perfectionism. Reaching this point of conviction is extraordinarily liberating, too, for it frees us from the compulsion of thinking we *have* to find situations that perfectly match our ideals. Yet it usually takes some careful reflection on biblical teaching to make this shift in outlook, for it differs from the idealistic notions so frequently taught in Christian circles. How often we hear statements like these preached:

"God has a perfect plan for your life, so make certain your choices reflect it."

"Don't marry someone whom you could possibly live without."

"If you have any doubts whatever about a decision, don't go ahead."

Scripture, though, never encourages such a perfectionist mentality in making our major life choices. Christ alone can perfectly meet our needs in any area, and any situation which purports to do so would become an idol to us. Also, learning to live happily even though some of our needs remain unmet is part of the secret of abundant Christian living. Having ideals for our choices is critical, yet setting them too high can thwart God's best for us as fully as setting them too low.

Why Our Expectations Defeat Us
What makes us prone to unreasonable ideals? Unhealthy perfectionism sometimes has its roots in an abusive or difficult family background. If my parents were constantly critical of me, I may have absorbed their overly demanding attitude. Consequently, I'm more inclined to see the faults in situations than the benefits. I'm also programmed to think that less-than-perfect in life is not acceptable. I feel uncomfortable—even edgy—in circumstances that fall short of my surrealistic standards.

The poor self-esteem that often results from an unsupportive upbringing can contribute to unwholesome perfectionism in two other ways. I may compensate for feelings of inferiority by taking refuge in fantasies. I may set my heart on realizing certain goals in career, lifestyle, relationships or spiritual life that are completely unrealistic and out of line with God's intentions for my life.

Focusing on my hope of attaining these dreams can momentarily inflate my self-worth and quell the pain inflicted by my past. My obsession with them, though, can keep me from appreciating the value of real-life opportunities God brings my way.

Low self-esteem may also lead me to despise opportunities which are available simply because they are open *to me.* I may conclude that anyone who is interested in me romantically, for instance, is not someone I could be attracted to. In *Smart Women, Foolish Choices,* Connell Cowan and Melvyn Kinder observe that many women equate romantic love with "longing," or craving for a relationship that is unobtainable. Women who confuse longing with love find it difficult to feel "in love" if their feelings toward a man are reciprocated. They associate love not with "having" but with "wanting." . . . Unless they recognize and change this pattern, they continue to play out this no-win game. . . . Women may resolve such internal conflicts by continually seeking out men who are unavailable. Because their love for such men is not reciprocated, these women can remain in that exquisitely miserable state of longing.

Nice men are not elusive, unknown, or mysterious. They're right there. They are predictable. They call when they say they will. And yet these men are often passed over because they don't stimulate that sense of longing so often linked with the feeling of being in love.[1]

Although Cowan and Kinder focus mainly on women's conflicts, I find that men are just as prone to the romantic idealizing these therapists talk about. Both men and women from unsupportive family backgrounds often look unfairly to romantic relationships to fill a void and are prone to think that unattainable relationships are more enticing than available ones.

While a difficult family background can foster an overcritical attitude or a tendency to take solace in dreams, many people from supportive families develop these same inclinations. Loving parents who go too far shielding a child from challenges or indulging him with material benefits may set him up to expect too much from life. Once grown, he finds it difficult to adjust to relationships and circumstances which seem less perfect than he experienced growing up.

Even if parents do not spoil a child, she may still grow to idolize her parents' relationship or certain factors in their life, then compare her own opportunities unfairly to her parents' model. The tendency to make such comparisons is extremely common in romantic relationships and contributes to commitment fear in relationships as greatly as any other factor. I've known many singles in good relationships who are hesitant to marry for fear their marriage won't live up to their parents' example. Usually this concern is highly unfortunate, for God makes us each unique, and our needs in marriage may differ sharply from those of our parents. Still the temptation to compare our own relationship to our parents' can be considerable, particularly when theirs has been dynamic and strong. (Conversely, when our parents' marriage has been unhappy, fear of repeating their pattern may make us hesitate to marry.)

Transforming Our Ideals
If our family background has been abusive or dysfunctional, perfectionist tendencies we've developed may be obsessive traits. We may benefit from the assistance of a qualified counselor who can help us come to terms with our past and break with any compulsive patterns that have resulted. Moving beyond unreasonable perfectionism also involves reshaping our outlook. Those of us from less difficult backgrounds may merely need to make some changes in our thinking to conquer self-defeating tendencies. Regardless of our background, we each will benefit greatly from making the effort to modify unrealistic ideals.

Our effort to overcome commitment fear should begin with confronting our perfectionism. We should look carefully at how unreasonable standards may be keeping us from accepting God's provision for our needs and how our expectations need to be adjusted. We want to be able to recognize good opportunities without compromising the ideals Christ sees as important.

In the remainder of this chapter we'll consider four principles for recognizing God's best when it seems less than perfect from our end. In the next chapter we'll look more closely at the remarkable benefit of making tradeoffs.

1. Let Go of Obsessive Concern for Guidance
While I've heard many stories about people who were excessively

concerned with knowing God's will, one stands out above the rest. Robert was a member of a church which taught an obsessive concept of guidance. Members were exhorted to seek God's will in all the small details of life. Uncertain about whether to get out of bed in the morning? Pray for guidance. Once you're up, ask God's direction about which socks to put on, which cereal to eat, which route to take to work, which parking place to choose—about all the particulars of the day.

Robert tried diligently to follow this practice but was constantly frustrated by a lack of clear guidance. Things finally came to a head for him when he collapsed in a supermarket one day and fell to the floor screaming, "God, is this really where you want me? Is this really where you want me?"

Most of us are quick to see the fallacy in Robert's outlook and in the teaching of his church. We know that God should not be expected to give special guidance for minor choices but wants us to grow through making them ourselves. Here he gives us the privilege of following our sanctified preferences (Gen 2:16). Stewardship demands that we not become too distracted by small decisions but use our best judgment and move on.

Many mature Christians, though, become highly preoccupied with finding God's will for major decisions. Those who fear commitment are especially likely to get caught up in an extreme concern for guidance, one that goes well beyond the healthy concern we should all have. Their quest for perfect decisions begins with wanting absolute certainty they are in God's will. And their obsession—and frustration level—often matches that of Robert.

The search for clear guidance is usually well-intentioned, based on a conviction that God wants to provide it. Apart from moral matters, though, Scripture never encourages us to expect God to provide perfect certainty about his will in personal decisions, not even in major choices. It does teach that he has a perfect will for these decisions. Yet it never tells us to become absorbed in finding it. Rather, we are to pray for willingness, then use the gift of judgment God has given us and make prudent choices. While God guides us, his guidance comes subtly—usually unrecognized—as we go through the practical process of making decisions.

It's in this spirit that the Israelite king Jehoshaphat instructed judges he appointed: "The LORD . . . is with you in giving judgment. Now then, let the fear of the LORD be upon you" (2 Chron 19:6-7 RSV). He didn't tell the judges to expect direct revelations of guidance from God. He did promise that God would guide them through their normal process of exercising judgment, providing they revered God.

In the same way we're assured throughout Scripture that we can find God's will through careful decision making. To this end Paul tells us that we who follow Christ "have the mind of Christ" (1 Cor 2:16). Through taking responsibility for our choices we grow in ways that wouldn't be possible if God always made it easy for us through direct guidance.

Even in a decision as far-reaching as marriage, Scripture never counsels us to wait for special guidance from God before taking the step. Rather, Paul declares, "since there is so much immorality, each man should have his own wife, and each woman her own husband" (1 Cor 7:2). Paul's admonition in the Greek literally reads, "Let each man have his own wife and let each woman have her own husband." In this verse and throughout his lengthy instructions on the marriage decision in 1 Corinthians 7, Paul urges readers to take responsibility for their lives. He gives guidelines for choosing marriage or singleness and for deciding whether to marry when an opportunity is present. In all of his emphasis upon making a responsible decision about marriage, Paul says nothing about waiting for special guidance before going ahead. Instead he advises the person who needs marriage to avail himself or herself of a good opportunity.

The fact that God wants us to take responsibility for our choices comes as welcome relief to those of us who are tied up in knots looking for an unreasonable level of guidance. We're not expected to wait for perfect certainty about God's will but are free to take initiative. Far from forcing God's hand by doing so, we're fulfilling his intention that we become responsible decision makers. If we pray earnestly that our choices will reflect his will, we may trust that he will guide us in his will as we make practical decisions.

2. The Principle of Suitable Choices

Paul says nothing about waiting for special guidance in seeking marriage; he also says nothing about looking for the perfect spouse. He obviously wants Christians to use good judgment in choosing whom they will marry. But never in his teaching on the marriage decision in 1 Corinthians 7 does he suggest that we should wait until all of our ideals are met before deciding to marry someone.

I find it particularly intriguing that Paul simply assumes his Corinthian readers can find someone appropriate to marry. Their church was only about five years old at this time, and it had many problems. It was not likely a huge congregation, and the pool of potential marriage candidates was certainly small. In spite of these limitations, Paul doesn't counsel his readers to go on a search for the ideal mate or even to look outside of their church for a spouse. He seems to assume that many of them, at least, can find a good opportunity within the Corinthian church itself.

Did Paul believe that God has one ideal choice for each person he wants married? If pressed, he would probably have answered yes, given his emphasis on predestination. Yet Paul never recommends that we should dwell on this thought in our search for a partner. His counsel on the practical level can best be summarized not as, "God has one perfect spouse for you," but, "God will help you to find someone *suitable* to marry."

This is one of the most critical shifts in perspective we need to make in seeking marriage. If we're caught up in the belief that God has one perfect mate for us, we're likely to assume that this person—and the relationship—must *be* perfect. If we think, rather, in terms of finding a suitable partner, we're much more likely to see the marriage potential in a relationship with someone who, like ourselves, falls short of perfect.

Beyond the marriage decision, it helps to aim for suitable rather than perfect choices in all of our decisions. Thinking this way allows us to maintain good standards of judgment without being paralyzed by impossible ideals. Regarding work and career, for instance, Scripture never suggests we can find a perfect job. Our career can provide considerable fulfillment, and the Bible encourages us to take pleasure in our work (Eccl 3:13; 5:18-20). Yet a certain burden is always involved in work as well (Gen 3:17-19). We cannot escape this dynamic tension, even in the best job.

3. Confidence in Providence

Learning to think in terms of finding suitable opportunities is not our only need, though. We also need to be able to recognize these special opportunities when they occur. We who fear commitment usually need to become much more alert to the open doors God provides.

Nothing helps more to increase our awareness of them than a strong conviction about the role of God's providence in our lives. Scripture teaches that God is working continuously to provide us with good opportunities that offer solutions to many of the needs we face. We need to believe this as a matter of faith.

Subtle differences in how I think about God's providence in my life, though, can strongly affect whether I recognize the opportunities he presents or am oblivious to them. My belief that he has a perfect plan for me, for instance, may lead me to think that choices I make must be perfect. In fact, this conviction should lead me to the opposite conclusion. It should help me realize that he is providing excellent opportunities through situations that appear less than perfect from my standpoint. It should inspire me to see his best in my imperfect circumstances.

The fact that God is actively working out his plan in my life, in other words, means that many of the opportunities I face are indeed

golden ones. To wait indefinitely for more ideal circumstances before committing myself can show a lack of faith.

While the theme of God presenting good opportunities through
imperfect circumstances permeates Scripture, it is especially clear
in Jeremiah 29. Here we find one of the Bible's most treasured statements about God's providential role in our lives: "For I know the
plans I have for you, says the LORD, plans for welfare and not for
evil, to give you a future and a hope" (v. 11 RSV). God assures us
that he is taking profound initiative to work out an incomparable
plan for each of us.

But when we recall this verse, we seldom consider the context
in which it occurs. The Israelites have been deported to Babylon
and are severely depressed over leaving their homeland. They see
no good whatever in their current situation and are reluctant to make
any long-term commitments in it. Yet Jeremiah instructs them, "This
is what the LORD Almighty, the God of Israel, says to all those I
carried into exile from Jerusalem to Babylon: 'Build houses and
settle down; plant gardens and eat what they produce. Marry and
have sons and daughters; find wives for your sons and give your
daughters in marriage, so that they too may have sons and daughters. Increase in number there; do not decrease'" (Jer 29:4-6). It is
following this exhortation to take initiative to rebuild their lives
that God then declares, "I know the plans I have for you . . . ."

Because he has good plans for them, God says, the Israelites
should see his best in their present *imperfect* situation. They
shouldn't wait for more ideal circumstances before taking steps to
meet their vital needs. And God notes three major areas where the
commitment-fearful Israelites should take initiative:

• *to find suitable living situations* ("build houses and settle
down")

• *to find work* ("plant gardens and eat what they produce"—a
symbolic way of saying "be gainfully employed")

• *to find marriage and family life* ("marry and have sons and
daughters")

Strongly implicit in God's counsel to the Israelites is that he is *providing* good opportunities for them in each of these areas. Yet they won't find them by being idle or skittish about commitment. They must take earnest initiative to discover the best God has for them.

We who fear commitment should consider this passage and its implications often. It suggests the need for a fundamental paradigm shift in the way we approach our decisions. Rather than insist that a situation must prove itself flawless before we commit ourselves, we should assume that a good opportunity is very possibly one we should choose. Of course we should use good judgment and weigh each option carefully. But we shouldn't be too quick to dismiss an opportunity because it fails to meet all of our ideals. Appreciating God's providential role in our lives should increase our conviction that an open door may be his answer to our needs.

Take a typical relationship situation. Alice and Jon have dated seriously for three years and have a deep, caring relationship. Both are mature Christians in their late twenties, and each personally wants to be married rather than remain single. Yet even though they are very much attracted to each other, they cannot resolve whether to marry. Alice worries whether Jon will perfectly meet all of her needs, and Jon wants a clear sign from God before going ahead.

Jon and Alice should put the burden of proof upon why they *shouldn't* marry, however, rather than upon why they should. Apart from a compelling reason, in other words, they should choose to get married. The fact that God has allowed them to tie up several years of their adult lives in a serious romantic relationship is itself a compelling reason to consider marriage, particularly given the level of their personal need and the fact that neither they nor their friends see any red flags indicating major problems.

4. The Personal Growth Factor
One factor more than any other can help us see the value of opportunities we would otherwise overlook. It's the advantage these op-

portunities provide for personal growth.

Many underestimate the marriage potential in a good relationship because they are focusing solely on the issue of their own happiness. The question of personal fulfillment is important, to be sure. Paul clearly teaches in 1 Corinthians 7 that unless we have a fundamental desire to be married, we should stay single and enjoy the special benefits of being unattached. Scripture teaches, though, that God gives us marriage at least as much for our own development as for our fulfillment. In marriage he places me for life in a relationship with another imperfect human being. I'm also thrust into a variety of new relationships—with my spouse's family and, especially, with the children we raise. Through all of these encounters God stretches me and broadens me in countless beneficial ways. My compassion for people is deepened. I learn to love and relate to others who are different from me and learn how to handle new challenges.

If you're in a good relationship yet cannot finally decide about marriage, it may be that your principles of judgment are skewed. Are you looking only at how the other person can make you happy? That is a dead-end question, for no individual can remotely begin to meet all of your needs for fulfillment. Consider also how God may use this person to help you grow. Looking at a relationship from this standpoint can make a remarkable difference in seeing its full benefits and can even be the turning point in deciding with confidence to marry.

The personal growth consideration helps resolve many other difficult choices as well. Whether it's a job prospect, a living situation, an opportunity to join a church or serve within it, or some other option that seems less than perfect, look carefully at how this situation may help you develop as a person. Will it teach you new abilities? Will it help you better understand others who think differently from you? Will it help you develop better social skills? Will it help you grow in other areas where you need to mature?

We should each pray often that God will help us recognize the potential for growth in situations that otherwise seem less than per-fect. Even more, we should pray that he will deepen our desire to mature in all of the areas that he considers significant. Developing a greater thirst for personal growth can be the most important step we take toward breaking the inertia of commitment fear. It can give us the impetus to risk and to find joy in the challenges that arise in even the most carefully considered decision.

CHAPTER THREE

Tradeoffs Worth Making

Halfway through an intensive graduate program I lost my zeal. My pastoral heartstrings tugged at me; I wanted to get out of academia and back into people-centered ministry. I came close to quitting.

On Evie's advice I decided to seek counsel from the dean of students. When I walked into his office the next morning, he received me warmly and spoke with me at length, even though I hadn't made an appointment. After I explained my dilemma, he offered some simple advice: I needed to be willing to make some tradeoffs. It was a reasonable tradeoff, he said, to spend some "dry time" in exchange for the creative period that I'd already enjoyed. Besides, I would soon finish the program and could then begin to enjoy its benefits. When all of the angles were considered, the tradeoffs were certainly more than worth it.

As basic as this advice was, it hit a receptive chord with me. It was the right thought at the right time and gave me fresh heart. Once it dawned on me that it was okay to make some tradeoffs in order to complete the program, I felt comfortable doing so.

The concept of making tradeoffs has stuck with me and often

been the redemptive thought helping me over the hump in difficult decisions. Not that getting beyond the hump is always easy. As a perfectionist, I approach what I do idealistically. I think in terms of maximizing my potential and my fulfillment. Yet I always find that tradeoffs are needed in any significant step that I take. Initially, facing the need for them is a jolt to my idealism—a blow to the lie I've absorbed from my culture that I can "have it all." As it gradually sinks in that these tradeoffs are not only normal but desirable, they become easier to accept.

A critical step in recognizing good opportunities which seem less than perfect is learning to appreciate the value of tradeoffs. We instinctively resist the idea of making tradeoffs, for it smacks of compromising. We dread the thought of selling short our ideals or acquiescing to less than God's best for our life. As vital as the fear of compromising is, we must be careful it doesn't dissuade us from tradeoffs which are actually healthy and beneficial to make. Yes, following God's will should never entail compromising. It should never involve settling (agreeing to less than God wants to give us). Yet it often does require letting go of an unreasonable ideal for the sake of a reasonable one.

Or a lesser ideal for the sake of a better one.

Or an ideal that no longer fits us well for one that now better applies.

Such exchanges of ideals are essential if we are to realize our potential for Christ and experience the fulfillment he offers. They are almost always needed in decisions for marriage, career and other major steps as well. They are at the heart of what it means to make choices that reflect God's best for us.

Tradeoffs in St. Paul's Life
St. Paul was familiar with the need for making tradeoffs. In Philippians 1, for instance, he speaks of his desire to die and be with Christ. Far from having a suicidal urge, Paul simply recognized that the blessedness of living in eternity with Christ would be

unparalleled by any pleasure that he enjoyed on earth. At the same time, he saw advantages to his homecoming's being delayed. Staying on earth would allow him to invest his life in other people—to win some to Christ, to disciple as many Christians as possible. "If I am to go on living in the body, this will mean fruitful labor for me. . . . I desire to depart and be with Christ, which is better by far; but it is more necessary for you that I remain in the body . . . for your progress and joy in the faith" (Phil 1:22-25).

This same capacity to think in terms of tradeoffs even allowed him to experience considerable joy while in prison, for he realized the remarkable way God was using his internment to influence others. Not only was he having exceptional opportunities to tell members of the palace guard about Christ, but many Christians were gaining courage from Paul's example to share their faith in challenging circumstances (Phil 1:12-14).

Getting Specific

Let's look at some common ways that the need for making tradeoffs applies in our Christian walk today. While this list is anything but exhaustive, it includes some perspectives that are especially helpful to keep in mind when considering a major change in our life's direction.

1. Trading affirmation for creative accomplishment. We spend much of our energy trying to win the approval of other people. The desire to be liked, accepted and acclaimed by others is one of our central motives. For some it's the primary basis for everything they do.

This has its positive side. It spurs us to move outside of ourselves, to seek relationships and live a life which has value to others. It also opens us to being influenced by other people. Others sometimes see our potential better than we do. Their encouragement helps us find the resolve to take important steps of growth so that we will realize our potential.

But our desire for affirmation also has its negative side. We cannot please everyone. And invariably there are those—sometimes close friends or family members—who think of us statically and don't wish to see us change. They feel threatened if we grow, fearing that a piece of their own identity will be lost in the process. Their influence is deadening to our motivation, for we fear hurting them or losing their affection if we move forward.

Fortunately God has so constructed our psyche that we find fulfillment not only in pleasing others but in creative accomplishment as well. This fact doesn't jump out and strike us as quickly as the more obvious fact that it feels good to be affirmed. Yet when we have the privilege of completing a project or making meaningful progress toward a goal, we're often surprised at how strong our sense of satisfaction actually is.

Which is to say that it's a reasonable tradeoff to purposely decide to let go of some affirmation in order to be more effective in areas where God has gifted us creatively. Of course I'm not suggesting that you commit social suicide in the process. Telling others where they can get off is not the point. You will not benefit by snubbing nonsupportive friends and risking the loss of their affection. Yet if you lose *some* affirmation in the process of developing your potential or moving toward a goal, that's okay. Your overall experience of fulfillment will likely not diminish but increase.

And in the process you'll undoubtedly gain new friends who will appreciate you in your new role and affirm you in it.

2. Trading financial gain or lifestyle benefits for creative accomplishment. A related point is that it's worth letting go of some material benefits in order to increase our creative satisfaction in the work we do. This is not a natural adjustment to make. The underlying current in American society is that your personal worth is measured by the size of your salary, the type of car you drive and the neighborhood in which you live. And of course the implication is that as these factors improve, your happiness will increase as well.

Whatever pleasure does come from economic benefits pales in the face of the joy of using our most significant gifts and doing work which we're truly motivated to do. Still, as one psychiatrist observes, "it is extremely unusual in this society to make purposeful decisions to make less money."[1] This can be one of the most challenging and courageous steps we ever take.

Again, the tradeoff can be worth it, if in return you gain the opportunity to do work which better reflects your gifts and creative interests. While providing for your basic economic needs is essential (2 Thess 3:6-10), don't let this goal become all-encompassing. If you have the responsibility to provide for a family, remember that part of caring for family members is *encouraging* them. Since you can best encourage others when you're encouraged yourself, your work satisfaction will make a difference in your ability to love those in your family. This consideration should be weighed carefully along with financial benefits in thinking through any job option.

3. Trading professional activity for family life. This brings us to another tradeoff which has critical implications for those of us who are married. While it is wonderful to be involved in work that is creatively stimulating, we can become obsessed with work to the point that our family life suffers. When this happens, the quality of our work often deteriorates as well.

Canadian physician and stress expert Peter Hanson notes that poor family relationships contribute more to unhealthy stress than any other factor in our lives.[2] Tension within the family easily robs us of the creative energy we need for carrying out our professional work, homemaking tasks and other responsibilities. The converse is also true: good family relationships are a tonic inspiring creative energy and freeing us to be productive in what we do.

For people who are not married, the same holds true: the meaningful relationships in your life, whether with relatives or with friends, and particularly with the "family" that makes up your household, must not get crowded out by job or other responsibilities. Both the people close to you and you yourself deserve prime time and attention.

Time spent building my relationships with those closest to me doesn't have to be a distraction from realizing my professional aspirations. Indeed, it can be the most important investment I make toward those goals. The key is to strike a healthy balance here.

4. *Trading immediate pleasure or accomplishment for personal growth.* To return to a point emphasized in the last chapter, we take considerable pleasure from the experience of personal growth. Sacrificing immediate gains for the sake of long-term growth is very often worth the exchange. This is a vital point to remember when weighing educational opportunities against immediate options for employment, for instance.

Remember that our Lord himself spent thirty years of preparation for a ministry that lasted only three. Paul, too, after his dramatic call on the Damascus Road, retreated for a fourteen-year preparation period.

Billy Graham reflected at an evangelism workshop that if he had his life to live over, he would preach less and study more. He also remarked that if he knew he had but three years to live, he would study two and preach only one.

Again, the personal growth tradeoff is one of the most helpful considerations to keep in mind in a marriage decision. Unfortunately, it is usually the most overlooked. While God uses marriage to meet our needs for companionship, he also uses it to challenge us to grow into more compassionate, more sensitive individuals. Understanding this dynamic can simplify a marriage decision, in some cases considerably.

5. *Trading ecstasy for the comfort of a secure, supportive relationship.* On vacation this past summer I read Christian psychologist André Bustanoby's insightful book *Can Men and Women Be Just Friends?* Bustanoby laments how many leave a good, comfortable marriage in search of a new attraction. They long for a relationship as electrifying as the one with their spouse once was. They fall for someone new; all the moonstruck sensations are there, and so they marry again. Within a year, though, the romantic feel-

ings have mellowed and the relationship now seems, well, ordinary.

In a long-term relationship, Bustanoby explains, it is psychologically impossible to maintain the extreme romantic elation often present in the early days of getting acquainted. The initial exhilaration in romance—termed "temporary insanity" by another writer—is sparked by newness and mystery in the relationship, which by definition cannot last indefinitely. But in its place can come a quality of friendship that over the years continues to grow and offers extraordinary support and security. Bustanoby argues that it's well worth letting go of some ecstasy for the sake of this more stable benefit.[3]

This perspective is a redemptive one and, frankly, indispensable for a successful marriage relationship. It's an important outlook to keep in mind in choosing a marriage partner, too, for usually we place too much weight on romantic feelings. In the long run it's our friendship with the other that provides the most enduring—and satisfying—basis for marriage.

Looking beyond marriage to our other relationships, here too the exhilaration of a new friendship with a person who seems to have much to offer us can lure us away from more predictable but lasting friendships we already have. It's important to nourish our ongoing friendships and not drop them in favor of a new one which may or may not last. We must always beware of *using* people.

6. Trading security for adventure. At the same time, God does wish to bring a definite measure of adventure into our lives. The desire for new experience is recognized by psychologists as a basic human need. *Contrast* is essential to our vitality. While this must not be the basis for leaving a comfortable marriage for a supposedly more enticing relationship, it's often a good reason for making career or lifestyle changes. The tragedy is that as we grow older and become more comfortable, we easily lose our willingness to risk. We place security above adventure.

In his classic *The Adventure of Living,* Paul Tournier points out that we have an inherent need for adventure and stresses that this is a God-given instinct.[4] I agree heartily with his concern and recommend his book as the best treatment I have seen of the role of adventure in human life. We each need a certain balance between security and adventure. It's good from time to time to take inventory to make certain that the scales haven't tipped too greatly in one direction or the other.

7. Trading activity for time with Christ. Finally, I cannot speak of tradeoffs in the Christian life without saying something about our need for scheduling regular devotional time with Christ. Most of us are busy enough that a regular quiet time simply can't happen unless we're willing to put some other things aside. For many of us it means cutting back on our professional work or curtailing our other goals a bit. Here the greatest test to our faith often comes, for we prove whether we really believe that time with Christ is worth the sacrifice elsewhere.

Again, must I say it? The tradeoff is much more than worth it. Regular time spent with Christ benefits us in a multitude of ways—giving us increased vitality in what we do, building in us greater confidence of his presence and guidance, and opening us more fully to his work and provision in our lives.

* * *

To this point we've looked at how unreasonable ideals can keep us from appreciating good opportunities God brings into our life. I've suggested some changes in outlook which can help us better recognize God's best when it seems less than perfect.

Some people, though, resist commitment not because they fear their ideals might be compromised but because they fear they might actually be realized! It's the prospect of success itself that unsettles them. The fear of success is a major factor in many people's commitment anxiety. We'll consider this problem in detail in the next two chapters.

CHAPTER FOUR

Facing Our Fears of Success

When working on my first book, Knowing God's Will, *I labored* under the typical apprehensions of a writer—that I might not finish the project or find a suitable publisher if I did. But while my fear of failing was significant, I worried as much about what would happen if I succeeded! Writing a book means casting something of your private life and thought before the public, and that's scary. Would friends who liked me in my present role still like me in my new one? And did God himself want me to succeed? Perhaps I didn't deserve to have a published book. Perhaps he would punish me for seeking this level of accomplishment.

I recognize now that my anxieties about success were not unusual nor merely the fate of those who write, but the experience of many in every type of pursuit. Psychologists have shown considerable interest in this area of personal conflict, which they've dubbed "the fear of success." As specialists in the field never tire of pointing out, the fear of success is not the same as the fear of failure, nor just a misstatement of the latter. The fear of failure is the apprehension that you'll never reach a goal. The fear of success is being afraid that you *will* reach it but suffer disaster as a result. While the two fears are related in many obvious ways, they are distinct.

Specialists observe too that while the fear of success paralyzes some, we all experience it to some degree. The fear is often unconscious, revealing itself in dreams and otherwise inexplicable acts of self-sabotage. I know a woman who bailed out of a four-year college program only two weeks before graduation. Though her grades were good and only a few assignments remained, she claimed she had lost interest in getting the degree and saw no purpose in finishing. This was clearly the fear of success at work.

Yet often the fear shows up in more subtle forms of self-defeat: a migraine forcing you to cancel a cherished date; laryngitis before a vocal performance; shutting the door on a finger before a violin recital; staying up late and exhausting yourself the night before an important exam; forgetting where you put a vital document; coming down with the flu shortly after you begin an exercise program; getting an eye infection halfway through a writing project; backing a new car into a fire hydrant; taking too long to pack and missing the train; working too hard on a project and wearing yourself out.

This fear of success is at the heart of the commitment anxiety many experience, and it contributes to the problem for many others. It's often the major factor when one dreads committing to an alluring job offer or educational opportunity. It's the most common reason someone abandons a project or goal shortly before accomplishing it. It explains why some are hesitant to accept responsibilities within their churches even though they are uniquely qualified to fulfill them. Fears of success sometimes derail good relationships and opportunities for marriage as well. A typical reason: one believes he doesn't deserve the gift of marriage and fears God's retribution if he goes ahead.

A Special Problem for Christians
Christians unquestionably are more prone to fear success than most

people. Notable exceptions are those exposed to the positive-thinking schools. The tenets of positive thinking have been espoused throughout the twentieth century by certain authors, pastors and churches, Robert Schuller being the best-known modern spokesperson. Those who teach it stress the importance of success and the need to continually stoke the mind to expect it. "What you believe you can achieve" is the prevailing theme.

But while the positive-thinking philosophy helps many overcome their inhibitions, it also leaves plenty of damage in its wake. It fails to wrestle with the tension of being "in the world but not of it" or to consider how success balances with our need for self-denial. It does little to help Christians appreciate the reality of sin and their need for Christ's forgiveness. The result is that many positive-thinking Christians extol success too highly and fail to appreciate its dangers. And many are prone to think they can manipulate God to accomplish their ends.

While positive thinking has had an unhealthy influence at one extreme, more conservative Christian churches have done at least as much damage at the other extreme in imparting unhealthy attitudes about success. These churches have often failed to balance teaching on the evils of the desires of the flesh and the need for self-denial with the positive role of motivation and accomplishment in the Christian life. The result is a myriad of success phobics among modern Christians. Many Christians are convinced that God doesn't wish them to enjoy significant success. There seems to be more nobility and humility in failure—and far less hazard to one's relationship with Christ! A spiritual masochism results where the joy of suffering is courted in a way that's foreign to the spirit of Scripture.

In reality, Scripture has plenty to say about the positive side of success. "Whatever he does prospers," the first psalm declares of the godly person (v. 3). God has ordained each of our lives to certain accomplishment. Yet the fear of success can hold us back from God's best as greatly as any other inhibition or sin.

Peter's Example

We find an enlightening example of the fear of success in one of
the early encounters that Peter and his friends had with Jesus:

> One day as Jesus was standing by the Lake of Gennesaret,
> with the people crowding around him and listening to the
> word of God, he saw at the water's edge two boats, left
> there by the fishermen, who were washing their nets. He
> got into one of the boats, the one belonging to Simon, and
> asked him to put out a little from shore. Then he sat down
> and taught the people from the boat.
>
> When he had finished speaking, he said to Simon, "Put
> out into deep water, and let down the nets for a catch."
>
> Simon answered, "Master, we've worked hard all night
> and haven't caught anything. But because you say so, I will
> let down the nets."
>
> When they had done so, they caught such a large num-
> ber of fish that their nets began to break. So they signaled
> their partners in the other boat to come and help them, and
> they came and filled both boats so full that they began to
> sink.
>
> When Simon Peter saw this, he fell at Jesus' knees and
> said, "Go away from me, Lord; I am a sinful man!" For he
> and all his companions were astonished at the catch of fish
> they had taken, and so were James and John, the sons of
> Zebedee, Simon's partners.
>
> Then Jesus said to Simon, "Don't be afraid; from now
> on you will catch men." (Lk 5:1-10)

We would have expected Peter and his companions to be elated
over their unexpected triumph. Such an overwhelming catch of fish
is a fisherman's dream. They would surely want Jesus to give them
this success again and again.

Instead, they were taken drastically off guard by this sudden,
inexplicable achievement. They had grown accustomed to failure,
and success was a jolt to their comfort zone. They felt morbidly

unworthy of it. The miraculous catch of fish awakened them to Jesus' divinity and surely aroused the fear—deeply embedded in the Jewish mentality—that a face-to-face encounter with God meant death (Gen 32:30; Ex 33:20; Deut 4:33; Judg 6:22-23). They undoubtedly feared that as Jesus came to know them better, he would judge them fraudulent and use this same miraculous power to destroy them. Thus Peter's frantic appeal, "Go away from me, Lord; I am a sinful man!"

Jesus, in magnanimous compassion and grace, ignored Peter's self-defeating request (thank God he often ignores our prayers when they are misguided). He assured Peter and his friends that he intended *more* success for them, and on a more meaningful level. "Don't be afraid; from now on you will catch men," Jesus declared. Jesus' response clearly calmed the disciples' fears. They were so relieved to find he had positive intentions for them that "they pulled their boats up on shore, left everything and followed him" (Lk 5:11).

I'm certain that high among Jesus' greatest healing miracles was giving his early followers victory over their fears of success. He inspired in them the spiritual and psychological strength to bound beyond the inertia of their routine existence into the dynamic life of following him. In Peter the change was nothing short of revolutionary. On the day of Pentecost this man who had been plagued with inferiority stood up and forcefully addressed the multitude, convincing many to repent and follow Christ. Later even the Jewish authorities were astonished "when they saw the courage of Peter and John and realized that they were unschooled, ordinary men" (Acts 4:13).

If you're fearful of success, take heart. You're not alone. This is an area of struggle for many. Be encouraged: Christ understands your predicament. As surely as he has saved you, he can give you grace to overcome this fear and realize your full potential for him.

With that hope in mind, let's look more closely at what the fear of success involves. Certain apprehensions are common in anticipation of achieving a goal.

The Fear of Punishment from God
Some fear that God won't be pleased if they succeed in reaching a long-cherished goal. He surely knows they aren't worthy of this success. It will mean experiencing more pleasure and happiness than they're entitled to. Accomplishing their objective will make them more competitive with God, more like God. He won't like it. He will punish them.

In extreme cases some even fear that reaching a major goal will result in their own death. Psychiatrist Martha Friedman, author of *Overcoming the Fear of Success,* finds this apprehension common among Ph.D. and other advanced-degree candidates. Yet it isn't limited to academics, she observes. She describes one of her clients, a craftsman who fulfilled a life ambition of building a master racing boat. Yet he couldn't bring himself to apply the final coats of shellac, fearing that once he completed the project he would die. In this case therapy helped. Friedman was able to persuade the young man to take the step that terrified him. He not only survived but found finishing his project so satisfying that it spurred him to a new career: building.—and completing—master racing craft.[1]

The fear of being punished by God for succeeding, while obviously related to our spiritual perspective, seems also to be rooted in our psychological heritage. Many primitive societies have rituals of sacrifice established for appeasing the gods when one realizes personal success. And dream therapy reveals that confirmed atheists have subconscious fears of retribution from a God they consciously deny exists.

Our Christian teaching can either play upon this fear and aggravate it—as it too often does—or bring the answer of grace and abundant life which the New Testament proclaims. I'm not suggesting that the fear is unhealthy in all respects. We must always be on guard against success's becoming an idol. At the same time we should desire to see our gifts employed as effectively as possible for Christ. Generally, our best protection against success's taking on undue importance is not to forsake our gifts but to do whatever is necessary to increase our devotion for Christ. C. S. Lewis expressed it well in noting that our life is thrown out of balance not by loving things too much but by not loving God enough!

The Fear of Losing the Affection of Others

Another common fear is that others will love you less if you reach your goal. The complexes producing this fear can run deep and sometimes originate in childhood. If your parents constantly criticized you and belittled your chances of succeeding at anything, you may feel uncomfortable now defying their negative expectations. Your success would be a blow to their esteem, a snub of their judgment. You worry about the effect of wounding their pride—would they think less of you or withdraw their affection?

In some cases a child comes to believe that his failure contributes to family harmony. Parents who don't get along well may pull together over a child's problems. Following Calvin's suspension from junior high his parents stop ignoring each other. They spend several evenings together with him, helping him resolve his academic and social problems. While their attention is drawn to Calvin's predicament, they are not threatening divorce. The following week Calvin returns to school, promising to do better. His folks, relieved that the crisis is past, let down their guard. Soon they're bickering again, then refusing to communicate. Calvin is now getting less of their attention as well and feeling once more like the family's fifth wheel.

Through experiences like this a child discovers that his failure is rewarded more greatly than his success. His success does nothing to foster love between his parents. It may do little to win their affection, either, if they're too drawn into their own problems to affirm him when he's doing well. His failure, though, becomes a rallying point for family unity and compels his parents to give him the attention he craves. If this pattern continues throughout his childhood, his instincts may be tuned to fear success when he is grown.

Even if your childhood experience has not inclined you to fear losing others' affection through succeeding, it is still natural to worry about how others will react to your success. Friends have grown accustomed to you in your present role and appreciate you in it. Their personal identity may even have a stake in your not changing. Will they be offended if you succeed? Will they esteem you less? Such worries are common and stifle many from taking the steps needed to realize their potential.

The Fear of Outdoing Others

A closely related fear is that our parents or others we love will be hurt if we outshine their accomplishments. We're especially prone to worry about this if they failed in an area where we want to succeed. We may also wonder if we deserve to gain an advantage in life that they were unable to obtain.

If my father went bankrupt in his attempt to start his own business, I may feel guilty about realizing my career dreams. I fear my dad will be demoralized by my success or even envious of it. If my concern doesn't lead me to deliberately sabotage my goals, it may still rob me of the extra incentive needed to succeed.

In her fifteen-year study of the impact of divorce on families, psychologist Judith Wallerstein found that some children of divorce are unable to commit to marriage or sustain good relationships because of their uneasiness about succeeding where their parents failed. She describes the plight of Mary, a young single woman unable to resolve the direction of a four-year dating relationship:

> Mary's inability to break up or go forward in her relationship with Jim illustrates another dilemma in the queen of hearts game, in Mary's case one that is dominated by the ghost of her relationship with her mother. It is a complex problem with many strands.
>
> On one level, Mary does not want Jim to feel the pain of the rejection that she saw her mother experience. And she certainly does not want to be the agent of his suffering.

And at another level, Mary is fearful of surpassing her mother, of doing better in the world of love and marriage. This is a major issue underlying the fear of success that we see in many young women. It has its roots in Mary's continued strong identification with her mother, whose feelings of hurt and rejection have persisted. Mary feels unable to leave her mother behind, and it is no accident that when asked to close her eyes and conjure up any family figure, Mary thinks of her sad mother and begins to sob uncontrollably.[2]

Wallerstein also points out that women like Mary feel a strong need to rescue their moms. Such a woman feels responsible for her mother's welfare and places her well-being above her own. To allow herself the bliss of a healthy, committed relationship is to turn up her nose at Mom—the ultimate failure to commiserate with her sufferings. At the same time, such a woman feels strong compassion for her boyfriend and doesn't want to subject him to the rejection that her mom experienced. She is pulled by one instinct to commit to her partner, by another not to do so. This conflict of instincts explains the on-again, off-again pattern common in relationships of so many women from backgrounds similar to Mary's.

Interestingly, Wallerstein finds less evidence that men are deterred in relationships because of concern over surpassing their father's failure in marriage. In this case a man is more likely to identify with his dad's aggressive tendencies and be spurred to seek his best advantage in relationships. I find that men are prone to worry about outshining their fathers in career and educational pursuits, particularly when a dad is ashamed of personal failure in these areas.

Our fear of surpassing others can relate to important people in our lives beyond our parents. We may fear outshining the accomplishments of a sibling, friend, spouse, neighbor or coworker. We may even worry that our ministry for Christ to these people will be hindered if we succeed to a point that arouses their envy.

The Fear of Increased Responsibility
Many worry also that success will bring greater responsibility into
their life. This fear, of course, isn't without justification. Success
usually does mean additional responsibility. While we may long
for the benefits of reaching a goal and the greater influence it will
give us, we may fear that the additional challenge will tax us beyond our limits.

We can dread the increased sense of significance that will come
with our achievement, and the new responsibilities involved, on
another level as well: we may fear that we're not up to handling it
emotionally. Change in our self-concept is always unnerving—even
positive change. We may feel squeamish or embarrassed about taking on responsibility which to us signals a boost in status. When
working on several previous books I was troubled by the thought
that if they succeeded, I would have in one small way surpassed
mentors and teachers whom I look up to as heroes. I would then be
in a position of teaching them. That thought was unsettling. In my
self-image I'm still a student.

Some concern about additional responsibility can be healthy.
We always need to respect our physical and emotional limits and
strive to live within them. Yet even when further responsibility would
seem to fit well within our energy and motivational levels, we may
still feel uneasy about taking it on. Concerns ranging from simple
laziness to a fear of increased significance may hold us back.

The Fear of Insignificance
At the same time we can be hampered by a rather different concern—that what we accomplish may be of no ultimate significance
to human life anyway. Why bother to make the effort? So what if I
slave to put myself through college and pull top grades as an eco-
nomics major? So what if I land a good position with a corpora-
tion? What will I achieve that someone else couldn't accomplish
just as well?

What difference will it make if we have a second child? Billions of children have come into existence and died throughout history without making any impact on the world.

This spirit of futility is the continual lament of the writer of Ecclesiastes. As a writer I've sometimes been haunted by a statement made in that book millenniums before the advent of the printing press or word processors: "Of making many books there is no end, and much study is a weariness of the flesh" (Eccl 12:12 RSV). Whether in anticipation of success or in the wake of it, futility can plague us and dampen our sense of victory. Paul Tournier observes,

> Every success makes us feel more keenly, and more cruelly, how far we fall short of complete self-fulfillment. So for every book I read, there are a score of others that I regret not having read, and not being able to read. For every book I write, I think with regret of many others that I should like to write, and that I shall never write. For every patient I heal, I suffer at my powerlessness to heal others. Every friendship, every fruitful experience of human relationship makes me feel more sharply how far short we fall of the full fellowship to which we all aspire.[3]

I've suggested that the anticipation of success scares us because we fear it will bring more significance than we can handle. Now I'm saying it also arouses our fear of *insignificance.* We are complex psychological creatures and often experience conflicting fears at the same time. One moment the thought of completing a goal unsettles us because we fear it will elevate us to more importance than we deserve. The next moment we're sapped by the thought that even if we reach our goal, our achievement won't dent the world's problems.

Fortunately we can do plenty to get beyond these fears. In the next chapter we'll look at perspectives and practical steps that will help us overcome our apprehensions about success and gain a healthy motivation to succeed.

CHAPTER FIVE

Overcoming Our Fears of Success

In the classic movie It's a Wonderful Life, *Jimmy Stewart plays a* young man who goes through a serious crisis in managing his deceased father's savings and loan company. He comes to doubt his own worth to anyone and concludes it would have been better for the world if he had never lived. While he contemplates suicide, his guardian angel appears and reveals to him just what the world would have been like without him. The difference is remarkable. Because he wasn't there to save his brother's life when they were children, his brother wasn't around to save the lives of many sailors during World War II. And without his efforts to make loans available to working-class people, many had to bring their families up in sordid conditions.

The theme of the film is an important one, for it reminds us how easily we can lose sight of our importance to others and how greatly we can underrate the significance of our own lives. In fact, God intends each of our lives as a matchless gift to people.

Since the anticipation of success can fill us with fears of both significance and insignificance, we need to learn to hold on to two perspectives at once. On the one hand, we should remind ourselves that Christ has a distinctive plan for our life. He has given us a combination of gifts and opportunities as different from anyone else's as our fingerprints. The work we do may seem futile in a purely objective sense. Yes, we may take a job which could easily be filled by someone else. Still, our personality and mix of gifts will allow us to relate to certain people for Christ within our work in ways no one else is as well-equipped to do. And, in the mystery of God's providence, we'll be there to meet certain needs of individuals at just the right moment—needs that would go unheeded without our availability.

Tournier writes, "Nothing can be of greater assistance to a person who feels that life is too much for him than the certainty that God is interested in him personally, and in all he does, that God loves him and has confidence in him."[1]

Scripture gives us supreme reason for this confidence. The love of God for each of us is distinctive, personal in the most intimate and far-reaching sense. One of the primary ways God displays his distinctive love for us is through leading us in a unique, adventuresome, immensely fruitful plan that is designed for our life and ours alone.

But a sense of futility can keep us from taking the steps so critical to keeping pace with his will. We must remind ourselves constantly that God's plan for us is personally designed so that the work we accomplish will contribute significantly to what he is doing to meet a wide variety of people's needs. Others will be deprived of important benefits if we fail to act.

Seeing the Big Picture
At the same time, we should remind ourselves that ultimately our work is only one small part of the picture of all God is doing. We'll make plenty of mistakes, and the world won't expire as a result! Ultimately the work is God's, anyway, and we're forever in danger of taking ourselves too seriously. Martha Friedman shares her own

experience as a doctoral candidate:

I was on the verge of becoming a Ph.D. dropout when a wise psychologist said to me, "Why such a fuss? Nobody's going to read it anyway; it'll just gather dust on some college library shelf, and it'll certainly never be published. If you're meant to do important work, you'll do it after you get out of school."

I stopped obsessing, took a month off from my jobs, and finished my dissertation. While it's admittedly no major contribution to world science, it was a major contribution to my psyche. I had finished something important to me. It was . . . a matter of not magnifying what I was trying to accomplish.[2]

She adds, *"Minimizing the importance of a goal is an excellent way to reach that goal."*[3]

Sometimes before presenting a seminar on knowing God's will, I'm troubled with the thought that it's too much to try to handle a topic as far-reaching as the will of God for other people. I'm likely to forget something important, put the emphasis in the wrong place, lead them down a wrong path. God surely doesn't consider me worthy to be a spokesperson on this issue.

I quiet my apprehensions by reminding myself this is just one seminar, one short period for each participant in a lifetime of exposure to teachers and ideas. These folks are mature enough to know that every teacher has limitations and blind spots. Their eternal destinies won't be in peril if I state something less than perfectly. They are only going to absorb a small portion of what I say anyway! The speakers and authors who have touched my life most significantly have done so far more through their humanity than through the details of what they said. I have margin for error; God will apply the truth necessary to each life.

We each need to work at achieving a healthy balance in the way we perceive our work. We need to know that what we do is significant; yet we must remember that we're instruments of a God who uses our weaknesses as effectively as our strengths. In Christ we can achieve this balance, for we know that while our work is an important part of the help he extends to the world, he doesn't ultimately *depend* upon us but graciously uses our availability. With this knowledge, we can serve in a spirit of joyous victory, not defeat.

But What Will Others Think?

In developing a healthy outlook on success, we also need to come to terms with our concern about how others will react to our success. The perception that others don't want us to succeed sometimes has basis. People don't always like it when we change. They may withdraw their affection. But remember that God has made human nature remarkably resilient. We can bear the disappointment of lost affection if something positive takes its place. Again, it can be a worthwhile tradeoff to let go of some affirmation in order to experience the joy of using our gifts more fully. In addition, as we take steps of growth we best position ourselves to develop new friendships. In the long run we're happier in relationships with those who desire God's best for us than with those who insist we conform to their still-life pictures.

But what about the fear that our success will dishearten our parents or others who are discouraged about their own failures? The concern not to hurt others by outshining them can spring from compassion, respect and a genuine desire to promote their welfare. Still, it is always a case of assuming responsibility that isn't properly ours and indicates we've been drawn into a codependent mentality. Following Christ means learning to trust into his hands not only our own lives but others' lives as well.

If my success causes my parents or anyone else to feel dejected, they are basing their self-worth on the wrong factors to begin with. Rather than needing me to adjust my plans to their expectations, they need to grow personally. They will be fulfilled only when they accept God's unique plan for their own lives and learn to make the best of their own opportunities. Until they stop measuring their happiness against others' successes and failures, they are doomed to stay frustrated. I'm not helping them change by accommodating their unhealthy outlook; I'm causing it to become more deeply ingrained. I'll best serve them by refusing to let their attitude dampen my zeal to succeed. I should remember, too, that beyond these people, Christ calls me to love many others. My success will better equip me to serve their needs.

Practical Steps
Finally, let's look at some practical steps we can take to manage our anxieties about success.

1. The role of prayer. It is hard to exaggerate the importance of our personal devotional time as a setting for confronting our fears. We will benefit greatly by giving some generous attention during this time to quiet reflection. We need to dwell on God's grace and provision for our life, as well as stare our irrational fears in the face and recognize them for the straw men that they are. Make it a practice during your quiet time to prayerfully examine your fears of success and acknowledge their unreasonable nature. Remind yourself that God has put you on earth for the sake of certain accomplishments. You are not fighting him by moving toward your goals but cooperating with him, when these goals are ones he wants you to pursue.

We should also make a point of establishing our priorities and daily schedule during our devotional time. When I've resolved in prayer that I should spend my time in certain ways during the day, I'm able to go forth with the confidence that I'm following God's intentions and not just my own impulses. Later, when someone asks, "Did you get everything done?" I can say, "No, but I got done what the Lord wanted me to." The conviction of God's call, more than any factor, strengthens our motivation and quells our fears of both failure and success.

It is helpful, too, to pray for victory over the fear of success. If your fears of success are severe, you should devote some concerted time to praying about the problem. Set aside a special time to ask for God's healing. Allow yourself an hour or longer to examine the problem carefully before Christ and pray earnestly for his help. Take heart in knowing that even though your fears seem overwhelming, God's grace is infinitely greater. He is able to bring unlimited resources to your aid. Scripture gives abundant evidence that God grants prayers for emotional healing. Often, too, he waits to see that we depend upon him enough to pray seriously for his help before he provides the full measure of assistance that we need.

2. *Help from our friends.* God's healing from our fears comes, in part, through the encouragement of friends, counselors and those in our fellowship groups. What makes the fear of success so unsettling for many is the mistaken perception that they alone suffer from it. It's therapeutic simply to find how universal the problem actually is. Seek relationships and, if possible, a support group where you can be straightforward in sharing your apprehensions of success. You'll undoubtedly be relieved to find that others have the same concerns. Pray for each other and encourage one another as you move forward. The renewed confidence that comes from this interaction can be tremendous.

If your fears of success have their roots in childhood traumas and a difficult home situation, I would urge you also to seek the help of a trained counselor. You should feel no more embarrassed to ask the help of a counseling professional than you would to consult a medical doctor for a physical problem. Take advantage of all the help you can get and, especially, of the *best* help available.

3. *Manage the benefits of success.* Martha Friedman recommends that those who experience success shouldn't try to appropriate the benefits of it all at once. It takes time for our psyches to adapt to change, even positive change. We need to be realistic about our own adjustment process and not make sudden drastic changes. For example, if I'm granted a large salary increase, I'll be wise to resist the urge to run out and buy a larger home. I may be happier

simply making some improvements in my present one. As Christians we're well schooled in the importance of not indulging ourselves with our material benefits but using them to help others in need. Friedman's point adds a further incentive for keeping our lifestyle within reasonable bounds. Doing so makes sense not only in view of our responsibility to the world but also *psychologically.* I don't mean that it's wrong for Christians to enjoy the benefits of success. Scripture extols the value of rejoicing in our achievements and enjoying the results of what we accomplish. The point is simply that *balance* is needed. We should remember, too, that if happiness is our goal, God has created us to find our greatest joy not in hoarding resources but in sharing them.

As you anticipate the possibility of success, dwell on how your accomplishment will help other people. Think creatively about how you may share your material benefits with others. If success does come, allow yourself to experience some reward for victory—that is important. But keep that reward within reasonable limits. The fear of success will be reduced and the joy of victory increased as you learn to manage the benefits of your success—particularly as you direct these benefits to others.

4. Keep the wheels in motion. Someone once asked Albert Einstein how he was able to cope with his great fame. He replied that he did so by continuing to work and pursue new goals. He didn't dwell on his success but kept his mind actively involved with new challenges. His example speaks to the importance of keeping momentum in our life.

Christ doesn't merely give us happiness; he gives us motivation. He puts within us the desire to be doing something significant with our life. The joy which he gives is not so much static and euphoric as it is dynamic and energizing. When it's experienced, it quells our fears and overrides them; our attention is occupied with the object of our motivation—the goals he's given us to pursue. Yet we don't experience this motivation sitting still any more than an automobile can be mobilized while in parking gear. Momentum is essential. We should do everything possible to develop a positive outlook on success, through reflection, prayer and interaction with others. Yet if our thinking isn't matched with action, we're unlikely to get the upper hand on our fears. We're far more likely to fear success when we're sitting still and dwelling on an unknown future—or wallowing in accomplishments we've already attained—than when our energies are engaged in moving toward a goal. The motivation of Christ is experienced most fully when our lives are in motion—not frantic, obsessive motion, but prudent, natural motion, toward goals which we've prayerfully resolved Christ wants us to pursue. It's through this motivation that our fears are transcended and we find the courage to become the person Christ has created us to be. And it's within this motivation that we discover most completely and convincingly the truth of the biblical promise of Nehemiah 8:10, that in the joy of the Lord is our strength.

CHAPTER SIX

Owning Your Life: The Subtle Challenge

As far back as Andrew can remember, his parents wanted him to become a doctor. Throughout junior high and high school his dad, a respected surgeon in the community, tutored him in science subjects and did everything possible to spark his interest in medicine. When it came to acceptance in a premed program, his dad's influence was decisive. Andrew was admitted in spite of borderline grades.

College was Andrew's first experience of living independently, and the freer university environment inspired him to consider other career options. After several sessions with a vocational counselor he concluded he was best fit for a business profession. He came close to switching majors. Yet as he pondered the effect this change would have on his parents, he decided to stick with medicine. The fear of disappointing his folks was simply too great, and in the end their expectations carried the day.

Andrew's parents also urged his younger sister to pursue a medical career. Yet Janet possessed a strong independent streak and fought the idea tooth and nail. In college she opted for a business major and today manages a retail department store. Ironically, Janet realized by her second year of college that she would prefer a career in nursing. Yet the knowledge that this option fell within the realm of her parents' wishes for her life was too great a deterrent. For Janet the crucial matter was to be her own person, and this meant avoiding any semblance of living out her parents' expectations.

Who made the more independent decision, Andrew or Janet? We're inclined to say that Janet did. She was the one who broke the bindings of her parents' expectations. Yet did she really? When we look closely at her reasoning, it becomes less certain that she acted freely. Like Andrew, she failed to follow the vocation she wanted. And like Andrew, it was her reaction to her folks' expectations that held her back. The difference was that Andrew felt compelled to follow these expectations while Janet felt compelled to rebel against them. In reality *both* acted from compulsion and not from freedom.

Andrew and Janet illustrate the challenge involved in trying to live independently of others' expectations. The goal of being our own person is a good one. Owning our life is essential to psychological health. It's a vital need for the Christian, for if I always feel obliged to please others' expectations, I'll not be able to respond fully to the Lord's will for my life. Owning my life is a prerequisite to yielding it freely to Christ.

Yet the goal of owning our life is also an elusive one. And unless we accept that it can never be perfectly realized, we're bound to frustration and a self-defeating mentality.

Many who fear commitment are fiercely concerned about owning their lives. Commitment fear is at heart the dread of losing control. For many commitment-fearful people this means fearing yielding control of their destiny to anyone. They can be unsettled just knowing that others *think* they are playing a role in their life. They may feel compelled to avoid taking any step which anyone else might claim credit for influencing. Yet their need for control greatly limits their options and may even lead them to sabotage their most cherished goals and dreams.

Whether or not we fear commitment at a chronic level, the urge to own our lives runs deep within each of us and is one of our most basic instincts. It can work either for us or against us. The challenge is to keep this drive within healthy bounds.

When We Try Too Hard

Janet demonstrates the greatest irony of the desire to own our own lives—the fact that when this desire becomes too strong it always backfires on us. The obsession to avoid even the appearance of living out others' expectations narrows our options considerably and may keep us from doing what we most want to do.

The problem can become pervasive. For some, even the vague sense that others might have opinions about what they should do is enough to keep them from doing it. Many who would like the benefits of attending church choose not to become involved, because they know others think they should be there. They stay away out of the urge to be their own person. Yet they are acting no more independently than those who attend faithfully out of social pressure.

This same mentality leads others to abandon good relationships and marriage opportunities. They are uncomfortable thinking someone else could claim credit for their happiness or well-being. They bail out of a relationship at the point when it becomes most promising, fearing they've become too reliant on the other for emotional support. They choose lonely independence over happy dependence.

Others strive fervently to act independently in all their decisions. If we're at all socially active, though, it's unlikely we can ever take any major step which at least some people are not hoping we will take. If the concern with being our own person is too strong, we become immobilized. There just doesn't seem to be any course of action which is genuinely independent.

Facing Our Suggestibility

We should not underestimate, either, the role of our own suggestibility. We tend to think only certain people will succumb to suggestion—the highly compliant person who can be hypnotized in five seconds, for instance. Numerous studies have shown, however, that each of us is far more suggestible than we normally suspect. Our outlook and mood are constantly affected by a multitude of influences around us.

As I'm working at home today, the weather is overcast and my energy is lagging. Undoubtedly this loss of zest is due more to the dreary environment than to any physical factor. But I can't deny that it may result even more from the fact that I've always *heard* that we don't function as well in bleak weather.

Which of us has not made a significant purchase in recent months and later realized it was prompted more by media hype than by good judgment? And even with our most far-reaching decisions, when we look carefully at what influenced us, it's often startling to find the role that others' opinions played. Sometimes a brief word of advice pushed us forward. A comment made in passing—"You'd make a great preacher"; "You've got a nose for business"; "You should marry that woman"—stuck with us and determined our choice.

If we're honest about it, we have to admit that it's very difficult ever to demonstrate that any decision we make is truly independent. We simply cannot erase our suggestibility. In spite of our best efforts to think independently, we remain surprisingly capable of being swayed by others' expectations.

Striking a Balance

Being our own person, then, is a more subtle challenge than most people realize. It can require some significant shifts in our outlook and approach to life. Here are six suggestions for beating the challenge.

1. Accept the reality of living in a world of expectations. If I'm to realize my potential for Christ, I must accept a priori that there will be times when doing what is best will mean doing what other people think I should do. They may even be rooting for me to do it. They may even imagine that I'm doing it to carry out their expectations. I'll need to remind myself otherwise, of course. But if I'm too ruffled by the problem of appearances here, I'll never get off dead center. Independent action will be impossible. The desire to rebel will make me a slave.

Accepting the inevitability of sometimes living out others' expectations is a vital first step in learning to own our own life.

2. Keep the desire to own your life within reasonable bounds. Aristotle observed that a virtue carried to an extreme becomes a vice. I've often noted that Satan seems to attack us at our strong points as much as at our weak ones. He'll take a noble desire, for instance, and move us to focus on it to the point of obsession.

The concern to own our lives is a healthy desire. Yet when it becomes excessive it's self-defeating. A *moderate* concern to be free from the control of others' expectations always serves us better than an extreme one.

You shouldn't want to let go of the desire to own your life any more than you would the will to live. Yet if you are obsessed with a need for control, you should strive to temper this drive. Remind yourself of the problems that occur when it becomes extreme. Ask God to give you a balanced concern for owning your life. Christ is on your side as you seek to keep this desire within reasonable bounds and will give you success as you draw on his strength.

3. Strengthen your desire to realize your potential and to become what Christ wants you to be. An important step toward keeping the desire to own our life within proper limits is to focus our attention more on other personal drives. Not only do we each have a basic desire to be our own person; we have a drive for personal accomplishment as well. Concentrate on your desire to realize your potential, and do whatever you can to nurture that desire. Dwell on the benefits that come from fulfilling God's plan for you—in work, personal ministry and relationships. As your desire for God's will grows stronger, you'll find it much easier to live with the reality of others' expectations and to know what your response to them should be. Paul is an interesting case in point. At first glance his attitude toward others' expectations seems confusing. He spoke fervently of the need to obey God over people, for instance. "If I were still trying to please men, I would not be a servant of Christ" (Gal 1:10). Yet he spoke just as earnestly about the importance of serving others through accommodating their expectations. "I have become all things to all men so that by all possible means I might save some" (1 Cor 9:22). We observe both extremes in his personal life as well. He went strongly against the counsel of others in pursuing certain personal goals. He proceeded to Jerusalem in spite of the pleas of numerous Christians who begged him not to court disaster. Once friends even gave Paul a prophecy of guidance, telling him bluntly that God didn't want him going to Jerusalem (Acts 21:4). Paul went anyway.

At other times Paul was surprisingly compliant. When he journeyed to Macedonia, he went in response to a vision of a man asking for his help (Acts 16:9). Paul and his companions undoubtedly expected to find a man active in ministry in Macedonia waiting for their assistance. Instead, they found a devout group of Jewish women who had gathered for prayer (Acts 16:13-15). One of them, Lydia, responded to Paul's message and accepted Christ. She then invited Paul's party to stay at her home, where they remained for the duration of their visit to Macedonia. Luke notes that Lydia "persuaded" Paul and his friends to lodge with her (v. 15). Paul was apparently unwilling to do so at first, perhaps wanting to search further for the man in his vision. Yet he allowed Lydia to change his mind. Here he showed flexibility and willingness to let God use someone else to influence his thinking.

Paul's varied responses to others' desires for him makes sense only when we understand his frame of reference. His primary concern was not to own his life but to do the will of Christ. He knew that following Christ would sometimes require going along with others' expectations and sometimes going against them. This isn't to say that Paul didn't cherish independence and control. He clearly did want to own his life. His desire was strong enough to protect him from caving in to unreasonable demands others placed on him. Yet it was not so extreme that he couldn't listen thoughtfully to counsel—and he didn't recoil from yielding to others' expectations when it seemed advisable to do so.

Paul's flexibility in dealing with others' expectations is particularly impressive when we consider how headstrong and inflexible he was before coming to Christ. He demonstrates the balanced attitude that results when we become intent on following Christ and realizing the potential he's given us.

4. Rebel by conforming. Another important point is that even when Paul did grant the expectations of others, he did so as *a free choice.* He was able to be all things to all people without capitulating. "Though I am free and belong to no man, I make myself a slave to everyone, to win as many as possible" (1 Cor 9:19). Because his identity was secure in Christ, he could yield to others' wishes yet still be his own person. His self-worth did not depend upon having to rebel.

From another angle, Paul *did* continue to rebel after becoming a Christian. His dogged personality remained intact. Yet he channeled his rebelliousness in redemptive directions. He rebelled against his own tendency to rebel. He rebelled against others' expectation that he would rebel. Many times he rebelled by conforming.

It helps if we who are obsessed with owning our own lives can recognize that others *expect* us to rebel. They expect us to break our commitments. They expect us to go against the expectations of others, even if it means defying our own best interests. They expect us to do the unexpected. If we must rebel, we should learn to rebel against *these* expectations.

God doesn't expect us to violate our personalities when we become Christians but to harness their energy constructively. We should rebel against any personal tendency which inclines us to sabotage our own dreams. We can follow the counsel of others, even fulfill their expectations, without sacrificing our integrity. Owning our life is an *internal* matter much more than an external one.

5. Manage your suggestibility. While we cannot negate our suggestibility, we can do plenty to manage it. In *The Person Reborn,* Paul Tournier stresses that God does not bypass our suggestibility in directing our lives but works through it to guide us.[1] Our aim should not be to avoid being suggestible, which is an impossible goal. We should strive, rather, to put ourselves in situations where the most healthy "suggestions" occur. Being around optimistic people who believe the best for us can make a great difference. So can exposing ourselves to healthy Christian teaching and worship experiences. We are profoundly affected by role models as well. I should choose to spend my time with people whose attitude and lifestyle I admire. I will be less likely to make that unnecessary purchase, for instance, if my friends are content with what they have than if they are lavish spenders.

6. Pray for wisdom. Most important, we need private time, quiet time alone with Jesus Christ—a point I want to return to frequently in this book. Appreciating our suggestibility helps us understand the need for personal time with Christ, where we give him an unhindered opportunity to influence our thinking. The benefit of such time in helping us know how to respond to others' expectations is unmistakable. When I've committed the day to Christ and sought his direction, I can go forward confident that he'll guide my decisions in his will. He'll give me sound perspective in the midst of the maze of expectations I'll confront.

Jesus himself found prayer indispensable in dealing with others' expectations. On one occasion he arose early in the morning and spent time praying. Immediately afterward, he went against the advice of everyone and left an eager crowd in Capernaum in order to minister in other towns (Mk 1:35-39). Following his intensive time of prayer in Gethsemane, however, he cooperated with the designs of the officials to capture him (Mt 26:36-56). While his decision was equally free in each case, his response to others' expectations was radically different. Again, we're reminded that God sometimes calls us to act against the expectations of others, sometimes to fulfill them. Through seeking God's direction in prayer, we can resolve this ambiguity.

Perhaps God in his design of human life has made the matter of dealing with others' expectations ambiguous enough that we would feel compelled to trust more fully in Christ to guide our life. It is through a relationship with him that we gain the strength and wisdom to fully become the individuals he has created us to be.

PART TWO

Managing Mood Swings and Runaway Emotions

CHAPTER SEVEN

Breaking the Grip of Mood Swings

Henri Nouwen was only six when he became convicted of his life's calling. He knew he should become a priest.

His life has been a history of astounding and diverse accomplishments. After ordination in 1957, he taught psychology and theology for many years in demanding academic settings, including Notre Dame and Yale. Today he is a parish priest serving a congregation solely of mentally handicapped people. He has successfully related Christ both to those who demand the most exacting intellectual argument and to those who are unable to relate to intellectual argument at all but can only respond to the gospel emotionally. He has also authored books that are among our most loved modern Christian classics.

Now well past midlife, Nouwen claims he has never suffered an identity crisis or vacillated in his conviction that he should be a priest responding to challenging ministry. He has always been assured of his calling and comfortable with his role.

I wish I could have this degree of confidence about my plans for this Friday night! I've already changed my mind several times about what I should do.

Gifted souls like Nouwen do exist, who are able to resolve even the most far-reaching decisions with astonishing assurance and never doubt their own judgment. They seem to have a surrealistic capacity to put their hand to the plow and not look back. Most of us cannot identify. We doubt our judgment on major and minor decisions alike. We know the pain of mood swings—of accepting a job with confidence, then several weeks later wondering if we've missed God's will.

I've personally known only a handful of people who have been able to march through life with the level of assurance Nouwen has enjoyed. That capacity for certainty is so unusual that I'm certain it's a divine endowment. Mood swings are the lot for most of us. We can take heart in knowing the experience is normal. It's not unusual to change our mind on matters ranging in significance from what toothpaste to buy to whom we should marry, nor to have second thoughts once these decisions are resolved. Most of us experience at least some shift of opinion and feelings on the decisions we make.

Fortunately, most of us are able to come to terms with the fact of mood swings. While we might wish our feelings were more consistent, we usually find it possible to move beyond our fluctuating judgment, make a decision and stick to it. For some, though, the problem is more serious. To say they are *tortured* by mood swings is not to state it too strongly.

I've counseled with some who have rethought a decision to marry so often that I've lost track of how many times they've changed their mind. One woman described the process to me simply as "hell." During a five-year relationship she often has felt mountaintop certainty about marrying her boyfriend, then despaired of her choice within a short period. Others I've known have vacillated similarly over decisions about career, church involvement or personal ministry. And buyer's remorse is not just an occasional moment of regret but a chronic tendency for some.

When mood swings reach this level, they contribute significantly to commitment fear and may even be its primary source. They greatly hinder our ability to make sound decisions, keep commitments and realize our potential for Christ. At this point simply tipping our hat to the problem will not help. A serious effort is needed to break the cycle.

What Triggers Mood Swings?
Let's look at why mood swings can occur even when decisions have been carefully made. Five major factors influence them. Any or all of these may affect the mood changes we personally experience.

Family background. The influence of our family background upon our emotional tendencies and patterns of judgment is considerable. For one thing, we instinctively emulate the attitudes and behavior we observe in our parents—a process psychologists term "identification." Even if we recognize these patterns as self-defeating, we may absorb them anyway. Isaac followed his father's practice of lying about his relationship to his wife in order to protect himself, for instance, even though the tactic had proven unnecessary and humiliating for his father, Abraham (Gen 12:11-20; 20:1-18; 26:7-11).

Parents who themselves are prone to chronic mood swings often pass the tendency on to their children. If either or both of our parents frequently wavered in their feelings about their spouse, their calling in life or other important matters, we may be inclined to respond similarly. In the same way, a parent who for some reason feels a sense of shame about sexuality may pass that along to the child, so that the child unconsciously works for self-protection by pulling away from romantic overtures.

Just as significant is how we ourselves were treated. If my parents were highly critical of me, often belittling my opinions and decisions, I may find it difficult to trust my judgment as an adult. While it may seem convincing enough that I should take a certain step, the voice of my parents rings in my mind telling me I don't have the ability to decide wisely. Two strong influences are swaying my thinking—my logical conclusion about what to do and my instinctive belief that my judgment is always mistaken. The result of this tug of war is that I vacillate constantly between conviction and doubt.

An abusive or unsupportive family background may make me prone to mood swings in a different way. If I didn't receive the love I needed as I child, I may be uncomfortable being loved and affirmed as an adult. I may earnestly desire a romantic relationship. Yet when the opportunity comes along, I feel strangely ill at ease with the experience of being loved and accepted unconditionally. Such exuberant affection is unfamiliar, foreign to my comfort zone. Again the tug of war sets in: I long for the relationship at one time, feel smothered or terrified at another.

An unsupportive upbringing can have a similar effect on my attitude toward career and other major endeavors. If I was never affirmed for excelling in activities I enjoyed as a child, I may feel guilty pursuing work or options I'm motivated for as an adult. Again my feelings will likely fluctuate. One day I'm attracted to the idea of starting my own business, the next I'm unsettled by it.

We who experience chronic mood swings may be reverberating more than we realize to the impact of a difficult upbringing. While we can do much to change the patterns that have resulted, understanding their source is a vital first step toward healing.

Biological factors. In addition to our upbringing, a variety of other factors influence mood swings and may affect us even if our family background was healthy and supportive. Biological influences are especially potent.

It's shortly before midnight, and I feel as if I've discovered hidden treasure. I've finally resolved a difficult turn of thought in a chapter I'm writing and have the perfect solution. I'm thoroughly pleased with my idea, certain it will edify my readers and bless the ages to come.

Now it's 7:00 the next morning. I wake with a start, sit up in bed and shake my head in disbelief. *What a stupid idea,* I muse. *How could I possibly have thought it would work? It will certainly confuse readers and take the book in the wrong direction.*

I've been through this pattern so many times that it no longer surprises me, though it always frustrates me when it occurs. I'm a night person, not a morning person. My outlook is affected by a daily biological cycle that never fails. The result is that I wax optimistic in late evening, skeptical in early morning. The effect is strong enough that my opinion may change significantly during this brief period: an idea that seems brilliant at midnight seems misplaced when I wake up just seven hours later.

We each experience a daily flow of energy and fatigue which even on our best days is largely consistent. The pattern varies from person to person. My wife's cycle is the opposite of mine: Evie is ready to hibernate at bedtime and wakes up with a full head of steam. All of us have daily periods when our energy predictably peaks and times when it just as reliably sags. The impact on our moods and perceptions can be substantial.

Fatigue always has a dampening effect upon our outlook, by robbing us of the energy needed to support optimistic thinking. Anything that contributes to fatigue—sleep loss, illness, stress, overwork, delaying meals or skipping them—can induce a mood swing.

Although the emotional impact varies among women, some are strongly affected by the hormonal changes associated with the menstrual cycle.[1] While men do not have a corresponding physical process which produces an emotional cycle, they typically experience a greater emotional letdown following sexual relations than women do.[2]

Biological factors affect everyone's emotional state. Interestingly, many who suffer chronic mood swings are not subject to stronger biological influences than others but simply react to them more adversely. Some are not sufficiently aware of how their physical cycle affects their emotions and thus take their mood swings too seriously. Others do not believe it is appropriate to discount a change in judgment merely because a physical influence induced a mood swing. They assume that a conviction about what to do—especially one that's in God's will—must be consistent and not swayed by any human factors. They feel obligated to wait for perfect certainty before taking any major step.

We don't have to look beyond Scripture, however, to find many instances when a person's physical condition affected emotions and judgment. Examples include the most mature and spiritually enlightened people in the Bible.

• Jesus himself became irritated when he encountered a fig tree with no fruit (Mk 11:12-14). His aggravation arose even though the tree was barren for a perfectly good reason: "it was not the season for figs." Mark notes a physical factor that influenced Jesus' emotions: "he was hungry."

• Following the elation of his incomparable victory over four hundred prophets of Baal and the restoration of rain to Israel, Elijah became suicidal upon receiving a veiled threat on his life from Queen Jezebel (1 Kings 19:1-8). Elijah had been stressed beyond all reasonable limits that day, through an extreme confrontation with the Baal prophets followed by a twenty-mile jog from Mt. Carmel to Jezreel.

• Peter's repeated denial of Jesus to bystanders in the courtyard of the high priest's residence seems incomprehensible at first (Mt 26:69-75; Mk 14:66-72; Lk 22:55-62). He had passionately insisted, a short time earlier, that he would die with Jesus. He had zealously intervened with a sword when the soldiers came for Jesus. Yet Peter was undoubtedly depleted from the events of that day—observing Jesus' agony in Gethsemane, confronting the soldiers and adjusting to the reality that Jesus had been captured.

Such examples remind us that no one is above being influenced by the physical. We cannot expect to gain a superhuman resistance to biological influences on our outlook. We must take them into account in weighing the significance of mood swings in our important decisions.

Temperament. Personality classifications abound, and it's beyond our scope to look at any of them in detail. Several points about temperament are indisputable, though. We are each gifted with a distinctive personality from God which is with us for life—the effect of nature and not nurture within us. Each personality has its strong points as well as its vulnerable ones. It's clear, too, that certain personality types are more susceptible to mood swings than others.

One of these is the analytical temperament. We who are analytical by nature tend to scrutinize all sides of an issue. We rehash our assessments over and over. Our conclusions may fluctuate, depending upon which aspect of a matter we're focusing on. When our analytical tendency combines with other factors, such as our physical cycle, we may be subject to strong mood swings and shifts of judgment.

The sanguine temperament is also susceptible to mood swings, but for a different reason. Sanguine personalities are feeling-oriented. They are strongly affected by the outlooks of those around them and the influence of their surroundings. The effect can be continual vacillation in a decision. Charlotte is often confident in the evening about her intention to marry Tyrone. She lives with her parents, who are both highly supportive of the relationship and eager for her to marry. During the day her conviction often crumbles. Her closest coworker disapproves of the relationship and is convinced Charlotte would be happier staying single.

Understanding your personality and its effect on your thinking can help you learn to respond to mood swings more appropriately. This is especially true when your personality by its nature makes you susceptible to them.

External influences. While sanguine individuals are more affected by these factors than most, we each are influenced by the people and circumstances in our life more than we usually realize. Our mood can be swayed by the weather, the attitude of the person we're talking with, the architecture of the building we're standing in or the associations we make with our surroundings.

Scripture abounds with examples of those whose mood and outlook were affected by their setting.

• Saul, king of Israel, could become inordinately depressed by the burdens of his office, yet often was incited to faith and optimism by the influence of music (1 Sam 16:23).

• David could be inspired to great reverence by the influence of godly people such as Nathan, but he was thrown into a moral tailspin when he caught sight of Bathsheba bathing from his vantage point on the palace roof (2 Sam 7; 11:2-4).

• Peter broke sharply with his bias against Gentiles following his rooftop vision and missionary experiences, yet was drawn back into the same prejudice through the influence of less enlightened Christians (Acts 10; Gal 2:11-13).

External influences often affect our own feelings and perceptions. Respecting them and making allowance for them is vital in breaking the unhealthy grip of mood swings.

God's peace is perfect—but the feeling isn't. A popular spiritual misconception also contributes to mood swings and makes it especially difficult for some Christians to put them in right perspective. It's the belief that if God is leading you to do something, you'll experience perfect peace. This is usually thought to mean that no fears or doubts will intrude. If you have any misgivings about taking a step, God is warning you not to go ahead. This assumption leaves many Christians stuck in the inertia of mood swings, unable to reach a conviction consistent enough to move forward.

While Scripture teaches that Christ gives peace to those who follow him, it never guarantees that we will *feel* peaceful before we take a step forward. God doesn't overrule our psychology. The peace he gives, rather, enables us to *transcend* our fears—to move ahead in spite of many hesitations. We may, in short, feel a mixture of peace and uncertainty at the same time, especially in the early stages of a major change. Many of us, too, are so constituted psychologically that we simply cannot feel peaceful *in advance* of a major step but only afterwards. Taking the step is vital to experiencing Christ's peace and opening ourselves to the full blessings of God. Simply recognizing that perfect peace is not required to resolve an important decision can help enormously to break the spell of mood swings. This insight can make possible a greater experience of faith as well, for faith in the biblical understanding is the courage to move forward in spite of less than perfect certainty.

Changing the Pattern

Beyond revising the way we think about Christ's peace, a variety of other steps can help reduce the intensity and influence of mood swings. They include these:

1. Gain a good self-understanding. Take a careful look at your life, and identify the factors which most obviously prompt your mood swings. Make a special effort to understand your personality. Take a standard personality test, or seek counsel from someone qualified to help you identify your personality features. Pinpoint your physical cycles also. Are there predictable times when your energy surges or lags? Do your moods typically change at these times? Your convictions about decisions?

Give close consideration to your family background. Did your parents' example or behavior in some way render you susceptible to mood swings?

Determine, too, what external factors most strongly influence your outlook. Are you affected by weather changes? Others' attitudes? Features in your surroundings?

A good understanding of why we experience mood swings helps us in two important ways. This insight alone is therapeutic, for our confusion over why mood swings occur is part of what makes the experience so disconcerting. In addition, this understanding enables us to better control our mood swings and reactions to them. We are able to identify which influences we can change and which we have to simply accept. We are also able to weigh the significance of mood swings more clearly in working through decisions and are less likely to be thrown off guard by them.

2. Accept your personality and physical makeup. An unfortunate result of chronic mood swings is that the experience can demoralize us. We imagine something is terribly wrong with us: we're psychologically unstable or even mentally ill. We despise our personality and the factors which make us prone to emotional shifts. This self-disdain robs us of the motivation needed to change, for we imagine we're cursed with a condition we can do nothing to improve.

In reality, our personality and energy cycle have been given us by Christ for extraordinarily good purposes. They are exactly the features we need to carry out his best intentions for us. This doesn't mean we shouldn't strive to recognize the vulnerable side of our makeup and do what we can do counteract it. Stewardship requires that we manage our life as wisely as possible for Christ. Yet stewardship begins with accepting—even cherishing—our personality and energy pattern as God's gift.

Appreciating them as God's gift strengthens our faith in Christ, sometimes radically, for our confidence that he can be trusted with the details of our life is boosted. This leads to greater trust that he will enable us to confront the problem of mood swings successfully. We are more inclined to do what we can personally to reduce their impact—and to take steps of faith in spite of them.

3. Manage those influences you can control. We cannot change our personality and shouldn't want to. We will not be able to alter certain features of our biological cycle either. We can always do much, though, to reduce our inclination to mood swings.

If watching *Lifestyles of the Rich and Famous* causes me to despise the home and neighborhood I usually love, I should stop viewing that particular program. If dour weather dampens my spirits, improving my environment indoors may help. A man told me recently that he had broken a spell of depression simply by increasing the light in his home. (Recent studies of the effect of light on

SAD—seasonal affective disorder—corroborate his solution.) If certain people have a knack for belittling my judgment or deflating my optimism, I should look honestly at whether it is possible to avoid them altogether or at least to reduce my contact with them. The influences we expose ourselves to can enhance good judgment or discourage it. This is the lesson of Psalm 73. The psalmist grew bitter observing certain successful but unscrupulous men who seemed to have an easy ride in life. He became despondent and "was a brute beast before" God. His jealousy subsided when he entered the reverent atmosphere of the sanctuary and took time to think things through from God's perspective. He was able to appreciate the plight of the people he envied and to see his own position in life more optimistically. The psalm is a good reminder, too, of the benefit worship and positive church experiences can have in helping us maintain a faith-centered outlook.

Any steps we take to reduce fatigue also have a stabilizing effect on our emotions. Basic improvements, like getting enough sleep, eating properly, exercising and keeping stress within reasonable limits can make a considerable difference.

4. Look at your pattern of feelings over time. We who are subject to mood swings face our greatest challenge when it comes to resolving important decisions. It's here that we also have to take our most courageous steps. Our inclination to mood swings can derail our most cherished goals and cause us to pass over golden opportunities. The point comes for each of us—even in decisions as monumental as marriage and long-range career plans—where we need to move forward even though some wavering of conviction remains. Our best understanding of God's will at these times comes from considering our pattern of feelings over time.

Fred has been dating Gloria for over three years and has often felt confident they should marry. Yet each time he has reached this conviction, doubts have set in within days and a period of ambivalence has followed. Fred has been through this cycle over twenty times.

When Fred looks honestly at the factors influencing his think-ing, he finds that he has usually become confident about marrying Gloria on weekends or holidays. These are times when he is well rested, away from the pressures of work and most able to think clearly about his future. Doubts have arisen when he is back at work and drawn into difficult assignments. Attractive women flirt with Fred on the job also, leaving him wondering if he's really ready to give up an active dating life to settle down in marriage.

Fred's conviction about marrying Gloria has come during times when he was most capable of good judgment. If he waits for per-fect consistency of feelings, he'll not likely marry Gloria (or any-one, for that matter). He would be wisest to follow his recurring conviction and decide to go ahead with marriage. Stability of emo-tions will more likely follow the step of marriage than precede it in this case.

We will each need to take a similar step of courage at major decision points if we're ever to break the bind of mood swings and realize our potential for Christ. Such a step is justified when, like Fred, we find that our conviction about what to do has resurfaced frequently and has usually come during our periods of best judg-ment.

5. Pray earnestly for God's help. We who regard mood swings as a serious problem should be just as serious about praying for God's help. Christ expects us to bring our most daunting challenges before him frequently in earnest prayer. The fact that God is willing to respond positively to such prayer is one of the clearest and most persistent themes of Scripture. In the case of mood swings he helps us by strengthening our resolve, giving us success in our efforts to deal with them, bringing gifted people into our life to encourage and support us, and providing numerous serendipities as well.

Even Jesus needed to pray fervently for God's strength as he faced his ambivalence about going to the cross. We should make it a practice during our daily devotions to pray for God's help in re-sponding to mood swings. We should ask both for greater consistency in our convictions and for grace to make wise decisions in spite of mood swings. And we should always ask for the courage needed to move beyond our confusion and take steps of faith. Following Jesus' example, we will also do well to occasionally set aside an extended time for praying for God's help. We should not regard such attention to prayer as merely catharsis but as one of the most critical steps we can take toward healing.

6. Don't be afraid to seek professional help. In confronting any personal struggle, the question always comes back to "Do I need professional help?" If my inclination to mood swings is rooted in a difficult family background, it may be triggered by repressed anger and deep feelings of inferiority. In this case the help of a qualified counselor will be invaluable and may be essential in coming to terms with my past and working through conflicts.

If my mood swings stem from a physical cycle I merely need to better understand and manage, or if they are inherent to my personality or the result of outside influences I can better control, I may be able to handle the problem on my own. When mood swings are chronic, though, there's often a variety of factors producing them. I may need the help of a counselor or qualified friend in determining the causes and my best route toward healing.

Some who suffer from mood swings are happy to take advantage of the best help available. Others are embarrassed to ask for help, particularly from professional counselors, or believe that seeking outside help implies they don't trust Christ adequately to solve their problems. Many who experience mood swings simply vacillate on this decision as they do on most others. Again, we shouldn't be any more hesitant to seek professional help for an emotional struggle than we would for a medical problem. And doing so is definitely not a sign of inadequate faith. Indeed, it may be an essential *step* of faith. We see numerous examples in Scripture of spiritually mature individuals who benefited greatly from the counsel of others whom God used to clarify their thinking.

If we're not certain whether we need outside counsel, we should err on the side of seeking it, at least initially, to determine whether we need further help or can manage the problem without it. Simply taking the step to get help is therapeutic, for it boosts our confidence that we can resolve an important decision in spite of mood swings.

CHAPTER EIGHT

Guidance and Intuition: How Reliable Are Our Gut Impressions?

A young man recently told me why he had broken off a relationship with a woman who wanted to marry him. "Everything about the relationship was perfect," Dan said. 'We were extremely compatible and a logical match. Yet the Lord told me we had to break up."

I asked Dan to explain what he meant by "the Lord told me." "I didn't hear a voice," he said. "But it was something much more than feelings. The Holy Spirit impressed on me directly that I was to break off the relationship. I simply knew in my own spirit that he was moving me. I've learned from experience to discern the difference between my own instincts and the prompting of God's Spirit."

His explanation of how he recognized God's will is a good description of what Christians sometimes call "inward guidance." The term refers to guidance through intuitive or mystical impressions. In the traditional understanding of inward guidance, God speaks to us directly through our inner impressions, which are sufficient by themselves to show us God's will.

We noted in the last chapter that some Christians rely heavily on feelings of peace in resolving important decisions. They assume God will give them perfect peace if he wants them to take a particular step. Not a few Christians, like Dan, take the notion a step further. They believe that God conveys all the particulars of his will to them directly through their intuitive impressions. These impressions—whether peaceful or not—must be followed, even if they contradict logical judgment.

This belief aggravates the problem of mood swings for many, who have to constantly revise their understanding of God's will in light of their impressions of the moment. Commitment-fearful Christians who depend on inward guidance face a further hurdle as well. They too easily read their uncomfortable feelings about commitment as a warning from God not to go ahead. Their impressions of guidance are often strongly at odds with what is best for them and keep them from appreciating wonderful opportunities God brings their way.

Mixed Signals

How, then, should we expect intuition to function in finding God's will? Should we assume God will lead us through inward guidance as part of our normal Christian experience? Can we expect our intuitive impressions to provide a reliable insight into God's will? Might God guide us through intuition *alone?* And is such guidance likely to fly in the face of our logical judgment?

Most Christians assume that God leads through inward guidance by itself at least occasionally. And many believe that this is his normal means of directing us.

Most of us, too, have either had positive experiences with inward guidance or know others who have. A man believes against all odds that God has shown him he'll be offered a job that a multitude of others are seeking. He applies and, to the amazement of his friends, is hired. A woman senses in prayer that God is revealing she will marry a man she hasn't met but only seen from a distance. In time a relationship develops and they marry.

If we personally enjoy such serendipities in our early days of walking with Christ, we may conclude that inward guidance is infallible and our best approach to finding God's will for a lifetime. Yet few of us live the Christian life very long without some cold-shower experiences that challenge any simplistic assumptions about guidance. I could fill many pages with stories Christians have shared with me about disappointing experiences with guidance in romance. A typical scenario: A man believes he has received a revelation from God about whom he'll marry, but in time it proves to be so much wishful thinking. I empathize with this humbling episode well, having gone through it twice as a young, single Christian!

The irony in such situations is that two Christians sometimes have conflicting impressions of guidance—one believing God wants them to marry, the other that he has said no.

The irony was not lost on Dan, the young man who told me God wanted him to break up with his girlfriend. As I talked with him further, he admitted that she was equally certain God had revealed to her that they should marry. It was the one factor leaving him unsettled about his own sense of leading.

This highlights one of the major difficulties with the notion of inward guidance—that it removes all basis for dialogue. If I believe God has spoken directly to me through an inner impression, I won't feel free to question that guidance. Nor will I be open to anyone else's insight. Yet Scripture declares that the wisdom from God is "open to reason" (Jas 3:17 RSV). Our impressions of guidance almost always need to go through an editing process. This is the point of the frequent admonition in Proverbs that there is strength in a multitude of counselors.

When it comes to trusting our perceptions of guidance, the advice of Scripture may be summarized: "Proceed with caution. Let your impressions season. And second opinions are usually advised."

Exceptions and Rules

I have no question that God sometimes does guide Christians through inward guidance alone. The testimony of notable believers to this experience throughout Christian history—including John Wesley and John Calvin—is convincing. Their examples suggest that when God guides in this fashion, it is usually for one of two reasons: someone is facing an unusual challenge and must make a decision in extreme haste (her life is in peril, for instance), or one is young in the faith and not ready to take full responsibility for thinking through decisions.

It appears, too, that God occasionally endows a Christian with exceptionally astute intuition. He may also give certain believers a spiritual gift for inward guidance, enabling them to discern his will through intuition more precisely than most Christians can.

But what about most of us? What should the ordinary Christian's expectations be about receiving inward guidance in most decisions? What is the *normative* biblical pattern?

The Bible records numerous instances where people took their feelings or intuition into account in a decision. No example can be found anywhere in Scripture, however, where someone regarded an inner impression as the *direct* voice of God, an *infallible* sign from God or the *sole* indication of his will. I have diligently searched both the Old and New Testaments on this point and have not found any clear example supporting the popular notion of inward guidance.[1]

Examples of direct supernatural guidance abound in Scripture, to be sure. They are often introduced by statements declaring that God "spoke" to someone or the Holy Spirit "led" someone to do something. On a superficial reading some of these might seem to be examples of inward guidance. Yet whenever a passage shows *how* someone knew God spoke to him or her, it is always clear that the person heard an *audible* voice. None of these examples is clearly a reference to inward guidance.

I am also unable to find any statement in Scripture which suggests that we should ever seek to understand God's will solely through inward guidance.

Understanding the Inner Light

This doesn't mean that our intuitive impressions have no role in guidance. Indeed, they have a vital function. But the way in which we understand their role has critical bearing on whether they enlighten us or mislead us. Generally, we do best to regard our intuition not as the direct voice of God's Spirit but as a window on our deepest feelings.

Psychologists observe that much of our mental process goes on subconsciously. When we experience an intuitive insight—an inspiration, a hunch, a warm feeling or instinctive urge to do something—it usually indicates that our conscious mind is reading what our subconscious mind is thinking. This insight can be critical, for our subconscious often processes information better than our conscious mind does. Our intuition, then, is telling us what underneath we most want to do or think we really ought to do. It's our best insight into what we perceive God wants us to do at this time.

We can trust, too, that if we're intent upon doing God's will, he is guiding our whole thought process—conscious and subconscious— including our experiences of intuition. Our intuitive insights are part of the enlightenment he provides us at any given time. Yet they are still more of a psychological experience than a spiritual one—an insight into our deepest thoughts and desires. They are our *perception* of what God wants us to do, a perception that may still need some room to develop. Our intuition is only as good as the information to which we've been exposed.

Not Locked In

This is a greatly liberating point, for it means we always have the freedom to question our instinctive impressions of guidance. We are free to seek further information—and this in time may lead to a new sense of intuition. Those impressions that remain with us, stand the test of time and most clearly reconcile with other indications of God's will are the ones we can trust.

A woman shared with me about how her understanding of God's will changed in a relationship she had recently broken off. When she first met this man she believed God was leading her to marry him. Her conviction was so strong that it felt like direct guidance from God. Yet during six months of dating she discovered that his relationship with Christ was shallow and he wasn't interested in growing spiritually. As this point sank in, her perception of God's guidance changed, and she grew convinced God didn't want them marrying. I appreciated her honesty, and her changing impression of guidance makes perfect sense once we understand how intuition functions.

Of course it can work the other way as well. In a survey of over one thousand happily married individuals, respondents were asked if they initially thought the person to whom they were now blissfully married was the right person for them. A full 80 percent responded no, that it had taken time for that impression to develop.[2] This helps explain why Christians are so often mistaken about initial impressions of guidance in a relationship. It usually takes time for a reliable sense of intuition about marriage to blossom.

Reliable Impressions
An enlightening biblical example showing the role intuition should play in our decisions is given in Acts 16:1-3. Here Paul selects Timothy to be his traveling companion.

> And [Paul] came also to Derbe and to Lystra. A disciple was there, named Timothy, the son of a Jewish woman who was a believer; but his father was a Greek. He was well spoken of by the brethren at Lystra and Iconium. Paul wanted Timothy to accompany him; and he took him and circumcised him because of the Jews that were in those places, for they all knew that his father was a Greek. (RSV)

We are told that Paul chose Timothy in part because he *"wanted*

Timothy to accompany him." Paul felt intuitively that Timothy was the right choice. Yet his impression was not based on blind instinct but on sound evidence. Timothy was a mature Christian ("disciple") who was willing to be circumcised for this mission. He had a cross-cultural background that uniquely prepared him for relating to both Jews and Gentiles. And Christians in at least two communities gave him high recommendations. The latter point is especially interesting, for it suggests that Paul made the effort to talk to others and get their opinions. He didn't make his decision in isolation. Through all of this research and weighing of evidence the impression emerged that Timothy was God's choice.

Paul's example of choosing Timothy is a good one to keep in mind in any important decision we face—whether it involves choosing a marriage partner, deciding on a career or job, or making any other major commitment. It suggests that our intuitive impression of what to do should emerge from carefully considering the best information available. If I'm about to take a major step solely because my instincts tell me God wants me to—even though I can't explain why—I have reason to stop and ask for further guidance. It is always proper in this case to ask God to give me a *reason* for taking the step, or else to change my impression of what he wants me to do.

Which is to say that we should seek God's will as much with our mind as with our heart. If we keep this in mind as our guiding principle in guidance, we'll be on good ground in our conclusions.

Special Encouragement for the Commitment-Fearful

We who fear commitment can also take heart that even if we cannot reach a consistent impression of God's guidance in a decision, we can still make a logical choice and know that we're not violating God's will by moving ahead. We don't have to be held back by the concern that our fears are a warning from God not to go on. We can look squarely at *why* we have a particular impression of guidance. If it becomes clear that commitment fear has triggered our impression, we can ignore it and let reason overrule our unstable emotions.

Whenever inward guidance seems to contradict our better judgment, we should stop and ask why. We'll probably find that we're basing our understanding of God's will too greatly on our feelings and missing his real intention in the process. In confronting areas where we instinctively fear commitment, we should let our reason carry even more weight than our emotions in deciding what God wants us to do.

At least that's my impression.

CHAPTER NINE

When Fear Takes on a Life of Its Own

Most people are not surprised to find that it's possible to fear commitment. Most are startled to find how severe the experience of fear is for some. Many are equally stunned to discover that they themselves are more than mildly nervous in the face of commitment. The opportunity for commitment ignites a panic reaction they feel powerless to control.

The level of fear some experience seems far out of line with any risks involved in committing themselves. It often seems out of character with the person who fears commitment as well—a person who may be bright, competent and fearless in other areas of his or her life. The intensity of some people's commitment anxiety makes sense only when we understand it as a *phobic* reaction. They have developed a phobia about commitment, as controlling and debilitating as the more commonly recognized phobias people suffer.

Phobias are extremely common. If you don't personally experience one, you probably know plenty of people who do. Yet most people do not understand the nature of the phobic experience very well.

A phobia is an irrational fear that has no relation to our courage and intelligence in other areas. Whatever legitimate reasons we might have for being afraid, our fear in the phobic situation greatly outstrips any risks we actually face. While it's sometimes possible to pinpoint the origin of a phobia, the factors which have given rise to it often cannot be determined. What is certain is that we have developed a *habit* of panicking in a certain situation. The tendency to panic has become ingrained and is now part of our lifestyle. And it involves physical reactions as much as emotional ones.

I identify well with the dilemma of phobias, having been a fearful flyer for many years. To this day I'm never as relaxed as I should be in an airplane, even though statistically air travel is by far the safest form of long-distance transportation. I confess to a certain fascination with the area of phobias as well. I've known so many talented, courageous people, with impressive life accomplishments, who suffer phobias in areas you would least expect.

• My friend Nick is so comfortable in airplanes that he easily dozes through flights at forty thousand feet. Once he boarded a plane, sat down and promptly went to sleep. He woke sometime later and, realizing the plane was on the runway, asked a cabinmate if they had reached their destination. She replied that no, the flight had been delayed and hadn't yet taken off.

This same Nick is so frightened of heights in open spaces that he cannot climb up on the roof of his one-story home to clean the gutters without getting dizzy.

• Belinda's case is just as interesting. She is a flight attendant with a major carrier and has flown countless international trips. I once asked her if she enjoys flying. She replied that she finds it thrilling and that takeoffs and landings are her favorite part. I felt a mix of awe and envy at her capacity to relish an experience I find so unsettling.

She went on, though, to mention a form of transportation that frightens her. Escalators. Unfortunately they are present in airports around the world. Her dread of them is so extreme she'll walk a mile if necessary to avoid using one.

• Another friend of mine, Margie, is a feisty elementary-school principal, highly respected for skillfully managing a challenging school with many international students. She has no qualms confronting students, teachers or parents who cause her problems. Most who know this assertive woman are surprised to find she has a morbid fear of bridges. She drives a circuitous route to work each day to avoid traveling the two Potomac River bridges on the Washington Beltway. This in spite of the fact that she already lives an hour's distance from the school.

• An example closer to home involves my wife, Evie. I've often been surprised by how unruffled Evie is with snakes. Because we live next to a large tract of woods, a snake will occasionally find its way into our basement. Unfazed, Evie gently sweeps the squirmy creature into a dustpan and transports it back to its natural habitat.

Mice? They are another story. Once when we were living in a two-story townhouse, I arrived home at 11:00 p.m. to find Evie sitting in our bedroom upstairs. A mouse had run across the kitchen floor at 7:00 p.m., she explained. Even though she had plenty of work to do downstairs, she had not returned to the first floor all evening.

Phobias. They defy reason, are often out of character with our personalities and can greatly complicate our lives.

Programmed to Fear

Phobias can result from a process military doctors have long termed "shell shock," more commonly referred to by psychologists today as "post traumatic stress disorder" (if psychologists can expand a two-syllable term to eight syllables, they will). The shell-shocked soldier is so worn down from horrifying battle experiences that he can no longer function effectively in combat. His fear of these events' recurring is so great that it overrules his better judgment. He constantly relives them in dreams and flashbacks. Unrelated sights or sounds—a car backfiring, a military convoy passing on the highway—can evoke the memories of battle and set off panic. Shell shock continues long beyond the time of military service for many soldiers and becomes a chronic problem. Psychologists now recognize that any traumatic experience can set the PTSD process in motion. Anyone who has suffered a major accident, been through a natural disaster or endured a personal tragedy may be shell-shocked by the experience. In spite of overwhelming odds that it will not happen again, one lives in fear of its recurring.

Rebecca loved sailing until one regrettable afternoon. She and two friends were in a sailboat several miles from shore near the mouth of the Chesapeake Bay when a wind gust seriously damaged their sails. She and her party tried frantically to row back to shore but couldn't make headway against the wind, which pushed them further toward the ocean and into increasingly choppy waters. The skies blackened, the winds increased, and an unpredicted storm began to release a torrent of rain. Their fate might have been sealed had not a fishing boat spotted them and given them a tow back to land. Today Rebecca is so frightened of boating she cannot sit in a rowboat tied at dock without a panic reaction.

A biblical character who suffered the effects of shell shock was Abraham's nephew Lot. The angels who escorted him out of Sodom just before destroying it urged him to escape to the mountains for safety. The gregarious Lot, apparently not eager to endure a life of solitude in the mountains, asked if he could flee instead to Zoar, a small nearby town. The angels agreed and promised they wouldn't harm that city. After watching a hailstorm of burning sulfur devastate Sodom, however, Lot changed his mind about where he wanted to live. "Lot and his two daughters left Zoar and settled in the mountains, for he was afraid to stay in Zoar. He and his two daughters lived in a cave" (Gen 19:30).

Lot had the assurance of angels that God would not lay waste the town where he lived. Still, his emotions overruled his reason. The trauma of seeing Sodom destroyed was too much. From that point on he apparently could not rid himself of the fear of burning sulfur raining down on Zoar.

Panic which we experience in the face of commitment can be caused by a PTSD reaction. If we've suffered a major blow in relationships in the past—the divorce of our parents, the failure of our own marriage, the breakup of a close friend's family, a stunning rejection in romance—we may be excessively fearful of the pattern repeating. Similarly, if we've experienced an unrelated tragedy soon after achieving a cherished personal goal, we now may inordinately fear the consequences of success. Painful past experiences in any area where we want to succeed may trigger panic when the need comes to commit ourselves.

Developing the Habit of Fear
While PTSD reactions account for some phobias, they by no means explain them all. A phobia can develop even when we've had no previous frightening encounter with a situation. I may absorb an irrational fear experienced by my parents or others around me through the process of identification we discussed. If my father fears elevators, I may develop the same anxiety-response as a child, then lock in to it for life.

In many instances it's impossible to figure out how and when a phobia began. I simply know I've long feared a situation—perhaps as far back as I can remember. The general process by which phobias develop, though, is well understood.

At some point in the past I first felt frightened about flying, for instance. Some long-forgotten incident may have incited my fear—a news report about a plane crash or a friend's story about a rough flight he endured. Whatever the cause, my anxieties were aroused. Since nothing happened at that time to dissipate my fear—a positive experience flying, for example—my fearful musings about air travel continued and over time became a habit. Certain physical reactions also accompanied my anxieties and caused the pattern of worrying to become more entrenched.

When we experience fear, we don't merely feel anxious but have predictable physical responses as well. This is a major reason defusing phobic fear can be so challenging. My fear of climbing onto an airplane is accompanied by tightening muscles in my arms and legs, for instance. Because I've long associated these physical reactions with the experience of feeling afraid, my realization they are occurring increases my fear and contributes to a panic reaction.

As our habit of fearing any situation develops, the point can come when merely thinking about the situation triggers a physical response, even before the emotion of fear occurs. At this point it can truly be said that our instincts are tuned to fear the situation and are all conspiring against us to make us afraid.

Commitment Phobia
Understanding the phobic process can be critical to overcoming the fear of commitment. Commitment fear often follows the pattern of a phobia in taking on a life of its own. Many singles I've counseled with have clearly grown phobic about committing to marriage. Although they talk about issues in their relationships they need to resolve, and questions about God's will which confuse them, their strongest deterrent to commitment is runaway emotions. No matter how carefully and completely the issues are addressed, they still feel afraid to move ahead with marriage. Some cannot pinpoint any issues troubling them at all but simply know they are seriously frightened about marriage. Carla, whose example begins this book, is such a case.

It is common for those who fear career success to also experience fear at a phobic level. One gifted office manager told me recently that each time she has found her way into a successful position she has purposely done something to anger her supervisor and get herself fired. The experience of success is so unnerving to her that she has to escape. Self-sabotage is the route she has chosen.

Some become phobic about church commitment and other obligations as well.

Phobias are most debilitating when they pertain to areas where we want to succeed. A fear of snakes may cause me some occasional inconvenience yet won't greatly affect my life, since my well-being doesn't usually depend upon having to relate to snakes. If I'm phobic about committing to marriage, or career, or church life, however, my fear may thwart me from steps I dearly want to take with my life. It may severely hinder my effectiveness for Christ as well and the benefit I can be to others.

Stopping the Panic Cycle

When fear has mushroomed into a phobia, it's not enough to merely approach the problem cognitively. Reviewing statistics about the impeccable safety of air travel, for instance, will do little by itself to reduce my fear of flying. I must also make a frontal assault on the problem of fear itself.

If I'm phobic about committing to marriage, my fears will not subside simply because others give me persuasive reasons not to be afraid. Fear has become a lifestyle. My instinctive reactions themselves need to be modified.

Because the emotion of fear is so closely connected to physical reactions, altering these responses can diminish the feeling of fear significantly. Mental discipline helps as well, particularly making a determined effort to halt obsessive thinking the moment it starts. Here are some steps I suggest in *Overcoming Shyness,* which are commonly recognized by phobia therapists as effective in combating the onset of fear.[1]

Practice abdominal breathing. When we're stressed, our need for oxygen increases. Typically we breathe more intensively but into our chests. This "thoracic" breathing results in part from our esteem for the military posture—"stomach in, chest out!" Yet in this position our lungs are not able to expand to receive their full capacity of air. The result is that we feel the need to breathe more quickly, and hyperventilation may occur. When under stress, we need to counter our natural tendency toward chest breathing. Let your stomach relax (and hang out if necessary!), then breathe slowly and deeply into it. Hold your breath for several seconds, then slowly let it out. The tranquilizing effect is remarkable. Continue doing this until your sense of control returns. *Relax muscles you tend to tense.* The next time you feel panic coming on, make a point of noticing your muscular responses. Do you clench your hands? Cross your legs tightly? Fold your arms? Tighten your stomach muscles? Push your toes together? Many of us who, like myself, have a frontal bite, clench our teeth. All these reactions increase our stress levels. The clenched jaw, in fact, can produce a number of other unfortunate side effects, including dizziness, distortion in the ear, migraines and facial pain.

Learn to identify your muscular reactions under stress, then make a conscious effort to counter your natural inclinations. Practice relaxing your muscles when you feel tense. Open your hands and let them hang loosely. Let your jaw hang limp. Resist the temptation to cross your legs or clamp them together. When relaxing the muscles is combined with proper breathing, the physical effects of stress and panic are greatly reduced. As a phobic flyer I can attest that these simple techniques have done wonders for reducing my uneasiness when airborne. They have helped reduce my anxiety in numerous public speaking situations as well. All of us can experience a considerably greater measure of control over our anxiety responses when these practices are followed.

Follow a healthy routine of rest, eating and exercise, and general management of your time. To return to a point stressed in chapter seven, we need to take sensible steps to eat properly, get the rest and exercise we need, and manage our time carefully. In general, anything that contributes to our physical well-being helps to reduce our general stress level. Like many people, I find that my appetite diminishes when I'm anxious or fearful. At the same time, when I neglect my normal eating habits my vulnerability to being anxious increases. If I'm feeling nervous about a trip or a talk, I think of eating as an act of discipline (at other times it's a wonderful celebration, but not now). I go ahead and eat a normal meal, even though I'm not particularly eager to do so. Again and again I find the simple step of keeping food in my stomach reduces stress.

We noted that after Elijah's exhausting encounter with the prophets of Baal, he panicked upon receiving a veiled threat on his life from Queen Jezebel. He retreated to a solitary spot in the desert and prayed that God would take his life (1 Kings 19:1-8). At this point God helped him in two ways. He sent an angel to make food for him. And he enabled him to sleep peacefully. After several days of such rest and relaxation his fear subsided and his motivation returned. "And he arose, and ate and drank, and went in the strength of that food forty days and forty nights to Horeb the mount of God" (v. 8 RSV).

In this case God healed a man who was severely traumatized by ministering to his physical needs. The lesson of the incident for each of us is clear: we can reduce our own vulnerability to fear through the way we manage our physical life.

Practice thought-stopping. Finally, we need to take a bold step of mental discipline to thwart obsessive thinking. Specialists who work with phobia sufferers recommend the practice of "thought-stopping."

When an unreasonable fear comes to mind, immediately yell internally (or externally, if no one is around), "STOP!!!" It may help to picture a policeman holding up a large stop sign, blowing his whistle incessantly and commanding you to halt. Be absolutely consistent in doing this every time an irrational thought troubles you. Insist that it cease and desist. Then immediately replace the fearful thought with a pleasant one. Think of a situation which you find relaxing or encouraging. Remind yourself, too, of God's absolute care for you, his desire for your very best, his forgiveness and his complete acceptance of your feelings.

The important thing, specialists point out, is being consistent and persistent in this response. Over time, when combined with other practices suggested here, thought-stopping helps significantly to change patterns of phobic thinking.

A Foundation for Other Steps

These steps will help us greatly to reduce crippling anxiety about commitment and other phobic reactions as well. If we are serious about conquering chronic commitment fear, we must recognize that our learned emotional reactions are part of the problem. We have developed a habit of fearing commitment. Fortunately, habits can be broken. We never have to be the victim of runaway emotions. God has given us much greater ability to defuse the emotion of fear than we normally realize. We are even capable of reversing our instinctive responses to phobic situations.

We should review these stress management techniques often and regard every onset of fear as an opportunity to put them into practice. With practice and persistence, they will enable us to break the cycle of panic and regain emotional control. As an effective response to the emotion of fear becomes part of our lifestyle, our other efforts to overcome commitment fear will bear much greater success.

There is one other important step that reduces our fear even when it's at a phobic level. I'm speaking of deepening our appreciation of the benefits that come from commitment. As our understanding of these benefits grows, our desire for them increases. Desire by its nature defuses fear. Our emotional energy is refocused in a positive direction, and we're less conscious of being afraid.

In the next section we will look carefully at the benefits of commitment. A greater respect for them will increase our incentive to make commitments and diminish the fears which hold us back.

PART THREE

Cherishing the Benefits of Commitment

CHAPTER TEN

The More We Want It, The Less We Fear It

As a young man, I feared flying so badly that I'd go to any lengths to avoid the unfriendly skies. When I had to fly, I endured the trip with white knuckles and knees that shook off the Richter scale.

Yet on one memorable occasion I flew without fear. No one was more surprised than I was.

When I awoke that morning in March 1974, I wasn't expecting to fly anywhere. I was managing the Sons of Thunder music ministry at the time. Yet I was no longer performing with this group with which I'd played guitar for over six years. I had requested this change, being newly married and afraid the band's travel schedule would disrupt family life.

I did miss performing. On this day I missed it especially, for the band was scheduled to play at Wheaton College that evening. We all felt especially honored to be invited to perform at Wheaton. Many of the pastors and Christian leaders we most respected were graduates of the school, and it was the choice of many from our own church who sought a Christian college.

Throughout the day I felt chagrined over missing this cherished concert opportunity. I kept wishing I could walk on stage with the band that evening. Then late that afternoon it happened, against the odds. Tom Willett, the band's music director, phoned to say that Dorian Lester, the guitarist, was stuck in Indiana with a disabled vehicle and wouldn't be able to make the concert. Was there any chance I could fly to Chicago and fill in? A flight was leaving Washington at 7:30, he explained, and the concert could be delayed until 9:30. With the hour gained flying west, I'd get there just in time.

Ecstatic, I told Tom I'd do it if I could possibly make the flight on time. That would be no small challenge. It was already past 5:00, and we lived in the remote suburb of Poolesville, Maryland, over an hour's drive from National Airport. Evie and I scrambled to pack, drove frantically to the airport, then waited less than patiently in the ticket line. We walked onto the plane at 7:29.

When the cabin doors slammed shut just after we took our seats, I felt not the usual surge of panic but elation. I was going to make the concert. For the next two hours, as the plane hurtled through the jet stream and bounced over air pockets, I felt no dread. I was too eager to enjoy the benefits this passage through the firmament would bring, too caught up in the adventure of beating the odds. There was simply no room in my psyche for fear that evening.

When Desire Overrules Fear
Two steps are critical to conquering any chronic fear. We need to work hard at reducing the fear itself and diminishing its impact on us. Yet we also need to make a sincere effort to *increase our desire to do the thing we fear.* My experience on that flight to Chicago is a classic case in point. My victory over fear that evening came unexpectedly—years before I learned any stress management techniques for reducing anxiety while flying. It taught me an unforgettable lesson about the role of desire in confronting our fears.

We shouldn't underestimate the effect of sheer desire in helping us break the pull of even extreme fear. Jesus understood this dynamic well and often employed it with his weak-kneed disciples.

An incident we considered earlier is a good example—the occasion when Jesus enabled his disciples to make an astounding catch of fish with one drop of the net (Lk 5:1-11). Fearing Jesus would use this same miraculous power to destroy him and his friends, Peter begged him frantically, "Go away from me, Lord; I am a sinful man." Jesus calmly replied, "Don't be afraid; from now on you will catch men." Not only did Jesus assure Peter and his companions they had nothing to fear. He also appealed to their deep-seated desire to accomplish something significant with their lives. The effect in quelling their fear was remarkable, for "they pulled their boats up on shore, left everything and followed him."

One reason desire helps us conquer fear is that we're incapable psychologically of experiencing positive and negative emotions at the same time. The woman who is drawn into rapturous music at a concert, for instance, is not feeling anxious about the financial woes that troubled her to distraction only a few hours before. Joy has replaced anxiety. Therapists who work with phobia sufferers stress this principle as one of the secrets to overcoming chronic fear. They urge the phobic individual to focus on pleasant and encouraging images when confronting the situation she fears. The fearful flyer is told to imagine a pleasurable scene—a balmy, relaxing afternoon at the beach, for instance—and to dwell on that picture while flying. As long as he is caught up in this soothing daydream, he is not obsessing about planes dropping violently from the sky and fiery crashes in cornfields. The peace of mind that comes from concentrating on these pleasant thoughts also reduces the sensation of fear.

It can be just as effective to dwell on the benefits of accomplishing what we fear. As our desire to gain these benefits grows stronger, we have not only greater incentive to overcome our fear but also less room in our emotions for the feeling of fear itself. When desire becomes strong enough, it effectively cancels out fear.

Stoking Our Desire for Commitment
No principle is more liberating to understand in our effort to over-

come commitment fear. Nothing helps more to break the bind of this fear than simply increasing our desire to enjoy the benefits commitment will bring. As our threshold of desire grows greater than our threshold of fear, we find it natural to move ahead in spite of fear.

If our desire to be married is stronger than our dread of being committed to marriage, for instance, our fear will not likely thwart us from going ahead with a good opportunity. We can reach this magic point either by decreasing our fear or by increasing our desire. Boosting our desire, though, is often the most effective way to diminish the impact of our fear.

The principle applies to all areas where we fear commitment. Gaining a greater appreciation of the rewards of commitment counteracts our fear of being locked in. If we want to overcome our fear of making a particular commitment, we should carefully consider the benefits that will come from committing ourselves. We should dwell on these benefits, recall them often and ask God to give us a deeper hunger for them. As our desire for them increases, we'll have a remarkable antidote to the paralyzing effect of commitment fear.

Perhaps you have read the material in the book to this point yet still feel you need more help in dealing with commitment fear. It may be that gaining a fuller appreciation of the benefits of commitment will make the difference. In this section we'll look closely at the rewards that come from making commitments and keeping them. Let me urge you to read these chapters carefully. Consider whether you've overlooked important benefits of commitment or not focused enough on them in the past. Ask God to strengthen your desire for these benefits and to help you keep them in the forefront of your thinking.

In this chapter we'll consider some pervasive benefits that result from all of our important commitments: peace of mind, greater enjoyment of our circumstances and a reputation for being trustworthy. In the following chapters we'll look at how commitment can help us realize our highest potential in career, relationships and spiritual life.

Clearing the Mind

It's early morning and I've got a bad case of buyer's remorse. Last evening I purchased a mattress for the daybed in my home study. Now, choosing a mattress is not exactly a monumental purchase decision on the order of buying a new home or car. Yet it's an important decision to me. I'll sit on this mattress constantly as I formulate ideas for articles and books. I'll nap on it often as well. My well-being and ability to help others through my writing will be affected profoundly by this crate of springs and stuffing under me. What a burden for any mattress to bear!

Last night the mattress felt perfect—firm but comfortable. This morning it feels too firm and not at all comfortable. When I stretch out on it, I feel like I'm lying on bedrock. I miss the familiar sag of the old block of foam it replaced. I couldn't sleep a wink on this mattress, I conclude, and I won't enjoy sitting on it either. I decide I've made a terrible mistake and must return this granite pad as soon as possible.

As soon as Mattress Discounters opens at 9:30, I phone and explain my predicament to the salesman. "It's no problem to bring it back," he replies, "as long as you haven't broken the plastic bag it came in."

Oops. That gigantic piece of shrinkwrap is now stuffed in a trash can outside my home. I remind the salesman that I've had the mattress in my possession for only twelve hours. I've spent no more than a few minutes trying to get comfortable on it. How much deadly contamination can occur under such conditions? He politely responds that health regulations prevent him from accepting it back under any conditions once the sealed bag is removed.

Stunned, I realize I'm stuck with this purchase. My first reaction is frustration. But soon after I hang up, a different emotion begins to settle in. Relief. I'm freed from the agony of having to reconsider my choice. The decision is final. I have no room to enjoy the luxury of buyer's remorse. I'll have to make do with the mattress and move on.

Very soon I make another interesting discovery. The mattress is beginning to feel comfortable. Perhaps it's loosening up a bit. Or perhaps it's my perfectionist standards that are doing so. Later that day I take a nap on it and sleep like a baby. Never since have I been troubled by that mattress at all. It feels natural and comfortable, yet not too firm a foundation. Thank God for little things, like health regulations which break the spell of buyer's remorse!

Commitment and Contentment

We who fear commitment often don't understand our own makeup very well. We fail to appreciate the relation between our contentment with a situation and our commitment to it. We imagine that contentment must come first and then commitment can follow. Yet more typically it works the other way.

My experience with the mattress reflects a process we go through in major and minor decisions alike. When we reach that magic point of knowing we're going to stick with a decision, our satisfaction with our choice improves—sometimes dramatically. Our contentment increases whether we purposely choose to make the commitment or—as happened with the mattress—are forced to do so. This change in outlook occurs for two important reasons.

For one thing, we're freed from the pressure of having to rethink our decision. We may be *stuck* with our choice, to be sure. Still, the release from pressure is significant. We've all had the experience. After a long, agonizing process we finally decide not to move, to stick with the relationship, to keep the car, to stay with the job. We thought we would be overwhelmed with grief over the option not taken. Instead we are surprised by relief—the sense of a great burden lifted.

If we're honest, we'll admit that the process of constantly

rehashing our decisions is painful. We who fear commitment suffer the same inner torment that haunts the obsessive-compulsive person. Like the compulsive individual who incessantly checks the iron and the front-door latch, we feel compelled to continually reexamine our most carefully reasoned decisions. Instinctively unable to trust our own judgment, we turn a decision over and over in our minds, always assuming our most recent conclusion must be wrong. The liberation we experience in firmly resolving a decision once and for all is not unlike the deliverance a compulsive person enjoys when finally able to let go of his numbing rituals.

Release from tortured thinking is not the only benefit that comes from deciding to stick with a situation for better or worse. Our ability to enjoy the situation also increases markedly. An important mental process takes over at this point—as much subconscious as conscious—where we begin to look for ways to make the best of the situation. We have much greater control over our fulfillment in any circumstances than we normally imagine. We can always take many steps both to adjust to them and to improve them. Yet we're much more likely to make this effort when we know we're committed for the long haul.

Our contentment in a relationship usually depends far more on factors we can control than ones we can't. We can determine to love someone, for instance, and as an act of the will decide to rekindle the fires of romantic love. Thus Scripture prods the married man to continually focus his feelings of affection on his wife: "Let your fountain be blessed, and rejoice in the wife of your youth, a lovely hind, a graceful doe. Let her affection fill you at all times with delight, be infatuated always with her love. Why should you be infatuated, my son, with a loose woman and embrace the bosom of an adventuress?" (Prov 5:18-20 RSV). We *do* have some say in the direction our emotions will take.

We can usually do much to improve the quality of a relationship as well. Yet our motivation to work at strengthening and enjoying a relationship is strongest, by far, when we're firmly committed to the other person. Commitment is a precondition to lasting, healthy romantic love.

Our happiness in other situations—including jobs, church involvement and living circumstances—can depend radically on our commitment level as well. You may be longing for a church that would meet your needs better, yet there are some good points about your present one too—you need to either move on or settle in. You may be restless in your job with its daily frustrations or lack of challenge; you should either initiate a job search or make a firm decision to stay. You may want a nicer apartment, then look at rents and decide yours is just fine for now. Decide—and *decide to stick to your decision.* Then you'll begin to experience the emotional rewards of commitment—peace of mind and greater capacity to enjoy the situation. We should ask God to give us a deep and earnest longing for these benefits. As our desire for them grows, our motivation to make and keep commitments will strengthen as well.

The Trust Factor
One of the most enlightening biblical passages on human relations describes a heated disagreement between Paul and Barnabas (Acts 15:36-41). The dispute arose over whether to take Mark with them on an upcoming missionary journey. Mark had traveled with them once before but abandoned them partway through the trip. While Scripture doesn't explain why Mark quit the mission, Paul clearly regarded his unexpected departure as a breach of commitment. This seems to be the viewpoint of Luke, the author of Acts, for he notes that Mark "had deserted them in Pamphylia and had not continued with them in the work" (v. 38).

Barnabas now wants to forgive Mark and give him a second chance. We may guess that Mark has repented of breaking his commitment to Barnabas and Paul and asked for the opportunity to prove himself again. Paul, however, is unable to get Mark's track record out of his mind. He's afraid to put Mark in a position of trust again, undoubtedly fearing he'll desert them once more if the challenges of the expedition get too great.

Was Paul right or wrong in drawing such a hard line with Mark? Scripture remains discreetly silent on the matter and doesn't clearly side with Paul or Barnabas. One point is indisputable, though. Paul— one of the most mature and respected leaders in the early church— formed a negative opinion of Mark because he believed Mark couldn't keep commitments. His dubious perception of Mark prevented Mark from realizing his dream of accompanying Paul and Barnabas on this trip. And it led to the most serious split between two early Christian leaders recorded in the New Testament.

Like it or not, others form impressions of us based on how trustworthy they think we are. Much of what feeds their perception of our reliability is our track record. If others know I've had difficulty making commitments in the past, I'll not score high on the trust scale. Similarly, if I've often switched jobs, left good relationships, changed churches or abandoned personal projects, others will wonder seriously if they can trust me.

If I'm at all concerned about realizing God's best for my life, I must take the trust factor very seriously. The best opportunities for me in relationships, career and other areas will come about only if others regard me as stable and dependable. Their willingness to support me and commit to me will depend heavily on their confidence that I can keep my commitments. My history with commitment makes a strong statement to others about my reliability and does much to open important doors or close them.

I don't deny that we can become too absorbed with the impression we're making on others. I've known Christians who have stuck with relationships, jobs, church involvement and other obligations way beyond a healthy point, fearing others would judge them unfaithful if they pulled out. They were too concerned about others' opinions in these instances. We who fear commitment, though, are usually not concerned enough about what others think about our faithfulness. This is a point where our consciences need to be stretched. We should remind ourselves often that a reputation for faithfulness will greatly enhance our prospects for enjoying the best opportunities Christ has for us.

The Old Testament proverbs speak often of the importance of faithfulness and the benefit of being known for it. For instance:

Let love and faithfulness never leave you;
bind them around your neck,
write them on the tablet of your heart. (Prov 3:3)

A good name is more desirable than great riches;
to be esteemed is better than silver or gold. (Prov 22:1)

A good name is better than fine perfume. (Eccl 7:1)

We should read through the Proverbs carefully and note the ones which most inspire us to take commitment seriously. We should review them often and allow the Lord to use them to deepen our longing for the benefits of a reputation for loyalty.

The desire for others to regard us as trustworthy is a good motive, providing we keep it in healthy balance. It inspires greater enthusiasm for making commitments and bolsters our motivation to keep them. We should work earnestly at stirring up this desire and keeping it strong.

Realizing Our Potential
Greater peace of mind, enjoyment of our circumstances and a reputation for trustworthiness are not the only benefits that come from commitment. There are significant advantages on the level of our personal accomplishment as well. In the next three chapters we'll consider how this principle applies in three major areas: career, relationships and spiritual life.

CHAPTER ELEVEN

The Best-Kept Secret of Career Success

Studies show that the most successful investors are often those who buy stock in major companies with a solid growth history and hold on to them for a long period. The value of these securities ebbs and flows frequently during this time. One is often tempted to sell when prices drop or make a quick profit when they suddenly escalate. Yet generally one does best to "hold 'em, not fold 'em" in these instances. Ironically, the investor who follows this simple, relaxed strategy frequently fares better than the one who constantly buys and sells, trying to maximize short-term gains.

This strategy which works so well for investors is an essential policy for planning our lives. Sticking with a situation through difficult times so often enhances our prospects for success in the long term. This principle is especially critical to our thinking in career decisions.

To say that finding our career niche is more of an art than a science is a considerable understatement. Nothing whatever is exact in the process. Most of us bump our heads many times, make many false starts and even change professional direction several times before finally settling into a work arrangement that is right for us. Even then, we may still shift jobs and even careers from time to time. All of this is normal at a time in history like ours. The job market is volatile. Corporate downsizing is a virtual epidemic; many face innumerable employment options, while others can find none at all; apprenticeship and family business are nearly lost traditions. It can require much experimenting to find our professional niche. Many legitimate reasons exist for changing jobs, positions and careers, and most of us will make a variety of these changes during our lifetime which have nothing to do with commitment fear.

Still, the point comes for many of us when long-term commitment to a career and job is essential if we're to fully realize the potential Christ has given us. The danger at these times for commitment-fearful persons is that they will not make the commitment needed or will leave a job position for the wrong reasons.

We can pick notable biblical characters almost at random and find a consistent pattern. So many of the ones who impress us most took time to find their stride in life. They changed directions at times, wrestled with God's will on occasion. Yet the time came when they settled into responsibilities and priorities to which they remained committed for a long period. They suffered plenty of frustration and disappointment as they pursued these ends. They also left many worthy goals untouched in order to concentrate on the areas where God called them. Yet over time their achievements were remarkable and their impact on others' lives highly redemptive.

Settling In

The advantages to our personal potential that come from long-term commitment to the same job or line of work can be considerable. They include these:

• *The opportunity to focus.* We have the chance to develop specific skills and areas of knowledge beyond the point usually possible in short-term employment. We are able to concentrate on major

projects which can be completed only through enduring persistence.
  • *Contacts with people.* Success in many types of employment depends upon having a large number of people engage our services. This is particularly true in sales positions, service-oriented jobs and most self-employment situations. Long-term commitment to the same job greatly enhances our prospects for making contacts with people and developing a clientele who will draw on our services repeatedly.
  • *Financial and lifestyle considerations.* Our best options for financial and lifestyle benefits often come from extended employment. The advantages that derive from a long-term job usually include a growing salary, increased retirement benefits and improved perquisites on a variety of levels, such as better vacation options. In many lines of work, such as teaching positions, job security also increases with each year of service.
  • *Promotions.* Similarly, long-term jobs often provide us with the best prospects for promotion to better positions which more fully make use of our skills and experience.
  • *Being part of a team.* For most of us, our greatest job satisfaction comes not merely from our individual accomplishment but from knowing we are contributing to the growth of a larger mission. Again, long-term employment usually provides the best opportunity for this to occur.
  A growing sense of shared history also results when we're interacting with the same group of people at work over a long period. Unforgettable incidents on the job, experiences within the corporate culture and legendary stories of the company's leadership become staples in the memories we share with coworkers and contribute to bonds of friendship that can last a lifetime.

Too Small a Place
A brief passage in 2 Kings gives us a helpful window on some of the dynamics involved in committing to a vocation or job for the long haul.

The company of the prophets said to Elisha, "Look, the place where we meet with you is too small for us. Let us go to the Jordan, where each of us can get a pole; and let us build a place there for us to live."

And he said, "Go."

Then one of them said, "Won't you please come with your servants?"

"I will," Elisha replied. And he went with them.

They went to the Jordan and began to cut down trees.

(2 Kings 6:1-4)

Certain men, whom the biblical writer calls "the company of the prophets," had committed themselves to minister with Elisha. The point came when they felt the setting where they lived and worked was too cramped. Their claustrophobic feeling parallels the frustration we experience in a job where, for whatever reasons, we feel hemmed in. Interestingly, though, they didn't quit their confining work situation but took initiative to improve it.

They told Elisha honestly, "Look, the place where we meet with you is too small for us." They didn't merely bemoan their predicament but suggested a solution—moving to the Jordan and constructing a larger building.

"Go," he replied. And when they pressed him to go with them, he answered, "I will."

How often we dread asking an employer for an improvement in our work situation, fearing we'll get a negative or evasive response. The prophets may have had similar fears as they approached Elisha. Yet his response was unequivocally positive. Of all people, Elisha would have had the right to claim that he alone knew what was best for his disciples and should decide himself what changes to make in their work environment. Yet Elisha allowed himself to be persuaded by their reasoning. God rewarded their tactful assertiveness, as he often rewards ours in work situations.

It is also interesting to observe the balance in the attitude of these men. Their request to Elisha was not outlandish. They asked for a larger building, which they would take responsibility to construct themselves. And the task would be accomplished with each of them cutting a single pole for support of the structure. The increase in space which they sought, then, was probably not monumental but incremental.

It is normal when we're frustrated in any situation to imagine that a major change is needed. Many times, though, a smaller modification solves the problem well.

Charlie imagined that the stress he felt at work meant he should look for a new job. His supervisor, however, wisely suggested some changes in Charlie's working situation, including a quieter office space, better lighting and a clearer definition of his work assignments. Within a short time Charlie's satisfaction at work returned, and he was glad he had not taken the more extreme step of looking for new employment.

A Risk Rewarded

As Elisha's prophets proceeded with their building project, one of them suffered a setback. The passage continues:

> As one of them was cutting down a tree, the iron axhead fell into the water. "Oh, my lord," he cried out, "it was borrowed!"
>
> The man of God asked, "Where did it fall?" When he showed him the place, Elisha cut a stick and threw it there, and made the iron float. "Lift it out," he said. Then the man reached out his hand and took it. (2 Kings 6: 5-7)

Commitment involves risk! As this man was cutting a tree, he accidentally lost the head of the ax. He was greatly concerned that he wouldn't be able to return this valuable tool he had borrowed. Elisha miraculously solved the problem in a way the man could not have predicted. As we carry out the responsibilities of any job, we'll inevitably encounter problems we hadn't anticipated. Yet when we're in the path of God's will, he often brings surprising solutions to the "insurmountable" problems we face. We shouldn't let the fear of meeting challenges discourage us from applying ourselves to our work and doing our best.

When Staying the Course Keeps Us on Course

There are many justifiable reasons for quitting a job or abandoning a career path. The challenge for those of us who fear commitment is that our reasons be appropriate and we don't merely take the course of least resistance. If you're considering a change in job or profession, look carefully at your reasoning, weigh your motives and be certain your expectations are realistic.

Are you thinking of leaving your present work situation for any of these reasons?

• *You are bored with your job.* Finding work that is creatively stimulating is an important goal. But do you have a history of quickly losing interest in jobs or projects you originally thought you would love? You may be placing too much emphasis on the initial rush of excitement that comes from a new position rather than the satisfaction of long-term accomplishment. Even the most rewarding job will have its dry periods and plenty of tradeoff between scintillating times and times when the work seems routine. Be careful not to become addicted to the honeymoon experience in work. Be certain you are not expecting a job to deliver more satisfaction than work by its very nature can be expected to provide.

• *You are overburdened with work.* Far from being bored in your present job, you may feel the challenges are too great or the responsibilities placed on you unfair. This can be a legitimate concern. Yet do you have a history of running from challenges rather than facing them? And are you certain you can find work elsewhere which is less strenuous but still provides the salary you need?

Most important, have you made an earnest effort to negotiate a better work arrangement with your present boss or supervisor? Don't run from the human-relations challenge here, which may be the most significant opportunity God is giving you to grow in this job. Confront it head-on, and you may be surprised to find that he gives you success. Be certain you have done whatever possible to improve your current situation before moving on.

• *The salary is inadequate.* Having a job that meets your basic financial needs is essential. Yet were you satisfied with the financial arrangement when you accepted this job? If so, why have your expectations changed? Are they reasonable? Or is it possible you are getting wants and needs confused?

It may be that your primary need is to learn to live more effectively within your means. Instead of looking for a higher-paying position, would you do better to put your energy into getting help with budgeting and financial planning?

Are you certain you can find a better-paying job? Will additional burdens be placed on you in the new position, and will the higher salary be worth the loss of personal freedom?

The salary returns of any job always need to be balanced against other benefits, such as work satisfaction and leisure time. Some people are happiest in a low- or moderate-paying job that places few demands on their creative energy yet leaves them maximum free time for other activities. I counseled this past week with a young man who is striving to develop a music ministry. Because he is employed as a driver by United Parcel Service, his evenings and weekends are free to devote to his ministry interests. He leaves his job behind at 5:00 when he locks up his truck; he never brings work home with him. The physical demands of his work contribute to his health and vitality yet do not drain the creative energy he would prefer to invest in music.

Be careful that you're not basing your self-worth too greatly upon your professional job and its salary. Remember that God sees your life in a much more creative fashion—as a broad combination of vocations and activities. While your job is an important part of that picture, it's merely one part. Some of us will accomplish our most significant work for Christ outside our professional positions. Let your job and the salary question fit reasonably into the total mix of responsibilities that God has called you to assume. Take your job performance seriously, working in a way that honors the Lord. But don't give your job more weight than it deserves. Remember, too, that God has created us each differently and has radically different plans for each of us. Far too often we base our own material needs upon what may be appropriate for someone else's lifestyle but not ours (Eccl 4:4). Certain financial benefits we crave may even be detrimental to what God wants us to accomplish with our time. For each of us, the critical matter is to grasp as clearly as possible the directions God wants us to take with our own life, then base our salary needs on that understanding.

• *The people at work are hard to get along with.* The social environment in some jobs is intolerable, admittedly. If you have been abused by someone at work, demeaned or criticized frequently by those you work with, you may have a good basis for leaving. The same holds true if you have been often blamed for problems you didn't create, your ideas and contributions have been consistently ignored or you have been unfairly denied promotions once too often. In some company cultures a newcomer is ostracized from the start by jealous coworkers and never accepted as part of the team. In other work situations the climate is so pervasively negative and pessimistic that even Forrest Gump would have trouble staying optimistic.

If your frustration with people at work is something less than one of these extremes, let me suggest two factors to consider. First, you'll encounter the difficult side of human nature wherever you work. It's easy to overlook this when you begin a new job, for people are usually on their best terms with you then. A honeymoon period often occurs. But within a short time things change, sometimes dramatically. Your office mates stop treating you like visiting royalty. You discover that they—like everyone else—are self-absorbed. They each have their idiosyncrasies, insensitive points and a tendency to get frustrated and discouraged. It may seem they are not affirming you nearly as often as you deserve.

It can be startling to discover that the folks you work with are, well, human. Yet this is the normal situation in the workplace. People are people. An important part of realizing your potential is learning not to be unsettled by the human traits of coworkers. Be careful you are not setting your expectations for the people you work with unreasonably high.

Consider, too, whether your own approach to people may be part of the problem. What does your past experience in the workplace suggest? Have you typically begun a job with high expectations of people but quickly been disappointed? Do you have a history of poor relationships with coworkers?

If your track record with people on the job is not good, don't imagine things will improve simply by changing jobs. In *When Smart People Fail,* Carole Hyatt and Linda Gottlieb observe that people most frequently fail in their careers not because of lack of skill but because they are unable to get along with others.[1] If you are concerned with realizing the potential Christ has given you, you may need to give serious attention to your style with people. Why not look at your present work situation as an educational opportunity? Look carefully at steps you can take to improve your social skills. Read a book on relating to people in the workplace; take a seminar or get counseling from someone qualified to help you learn how to better communicate. Determine to change your manner with people, and work hard at doing so. Sometimes simply learning how to apologize and affirm others more effectively is all it takes.

Instead of running off to the greener pastures of new employment, work on improving relationships in your present job. If you succeed, you will probably discover that this job has far more to offer than you realized. And any effort you make to develop your skills with people will benefit you in all of your work and social situations in the future.

• *The commute is too long.* I have the greatest sympathy for so many in the Washington area, where I live, who consume several hours daily in horrendous commutes to and from work. Your desire to reduce the time spent in travel to the job may be fully justifiable. Yet, again, remember that there are tradeoffs in every job arrangement. What compromises will you have to make in other areas, such as salary and job satisfaction, to find work closer to home? Will these sacrifices be worth it?

Is it possible that you can find ways to employ your commuting time more effectively? Can you study (if you take public transportation or ride with someone else), pray (if you drive by yourself), listen to educational tapes, work on a personal skill such as learning a language, or use the time to think through significant issues related to work or personal life? Be sure to look at all the options carefully before deciding to change jobs because of commuting alone.

The Bottom Line
In short, take extraordinary care not to make your career decisions impulsively. If you fear commitment, your tendency will be to choose jobs for the wrong reasons and leave them for the wrong reasons as well. Look carefully at your reasoning in any decision about accepting or resigning a job. Always put the emphasis upon making the best of your current situation before ever thinking of moving on. Place the burden of proof strongly upon God to show you why you should leave a work situation.

And constantly remind yourself of the benefits to your potential that come from long-term employment. Thoroughly consider these when you are tempted to change directions. Let the overriding consideration in every career choice be the desire to realize your potential for Christ as fully as possible.

The best-kept secret of career success?

Find what you do best.

Then do it.

And stick to it.

Stick to it.

Stick to it.

CHAPTER TWELVE

Going for the Gold in Relationships

Following a funeral service I conducted last fall, the widow of the deceased man spoke to me affectionately about her husband. "Jason always had difficulty expressing his feelings," she observed. "During the past six months, though, he made impressive progress. He was more verbal in sharing his feelings of love for me than at any previous time in our marriage. And it meant the world to me."

The improvement in communication which took place in this relationship did take time to develop. Jason was ninety-two when he died and Marion, his widow, eighty-nine. They had been married sixty-three years.

No, I'm not suggesting it will take sixty-three years for good communication to result in your own marriage. Yet I find Jason and Marion's example an inspiring reminder of two principles which operate constantly in our relationships.

One is that *the best qualities in any friendship or relationship take time to develop.* They are always the fruit of patience, persistence and long-term commitment. Those who jump from romance to romance miss some of the most cherished benefits of the male-female relationship. Those who always cut their friendships short miss rewards that can only come from continuing acquaintance.

The other is that *growth and improvement continue to take place in a healthy relationship, no matter how long it lasts.* One of the best rewards of faithful, earnest commitment in a relationship is that you always have plenty to look forward to, for on certain levels the best is always yet to come.

A Boon to Our Potential in Relationships
Commitment is critical to realizing our highest potential not only in professional life but in relationships as well. Not only does commitment contribute to the best experiences possible in relationships, but the support which comes from stable, committed relationships can do much to enhance our potential in other areas of life.

Our deepest longings for love, intimacy, support and sharing of memories can be met only in the context of long-term committed friendships and relationships. Developing a high-quality friendship can take what seems to be infinite time. You bear with your friend through endless difficult and challenging experiences. You bite your tongue countless times and forgive offenses without ever mentioning them. At other times you delicately confront your friend, raising an issue of concern. Yet you do so in a way that, far from undermining the friendship, strengthens its bond. You make time to be with your friend often, frequently sacrificing other options. You keep your promises to him or her, even when it hurts.

Over time the results of your forbearance become evident. You have built a strong ship that doesn't sink in rough waters and is an immeasurable source of strength and life to both of you.

For those of us who want to be married, a good marriage provides an opportunity for friendship, romance and personal growth unparalleled by even the best dating relationship. We who fear commitment usually place far too much value on the rush of excitement experienced at the start of a relationship. We may leave a good relationship for a new one in an effort to recapture this initial ecstasy. The moonstruck sensation present at the start of a relationship does diminish over time, admittedly. It is sparked by newness, mystery and anticipation—factors which lose their edge as the other person becomes more familiar. And it's always based to a large extent upon a fantasy image of the other which gets redefined in many ways as the relationship develops. Fantasy always seems more sensually explosive than reality. Always.

But hold on. Fantasy *seems* more enticing than reality, true. Yet the best-kept secret of marriage is that reality wins out in the long run. Reality wins, that is, if our *expectations* are healthy and reasonable. The problem comes when we expect the original exhilaration to continue indefinitely and then think less of a relationship when it doesn't. God has built us to find our greatest fulfillment in the lasting bond of friendship and intimacy that results in an enduring relationship. Yes, I'm speaking of a *romantic* relationship here.

A Worthwhile Tradeoff

In *Can Men and Women Be Just Friends?* André Bustanoby explains well the benefits of long-term companionship in marriage over initial ecstasy. He lauds the joy of being *comfortable* with your partner:

> Comfortable is sipping a cup of coffee with my wife as we slowly wake up in the morning and watch summer come to life around us. Comfortable is looking across the room at each other as we try to wake up and laughing together at being such zombies. Comfortable is waking up quietly— no need to say anything but just smiling and sighing. Comfortable is sitting in front of a fire in the wintertime, hearing the wind and watching the falling snow with someone who is easy to be with. Comfortable is sharing dreams and fantasies without fear of criticism or fear that my mate may take away from the relationship by indulging some private, unspoken need.[1]

Bustanoby also notes how unreasonable expectations can prevent us from experiencing this deeper pleasure that marriage offers:
The myth of happiness is destructive because it robs us of the greatest reward of friendship in marriage—comfort. We wake up one morning and don't feel any excitement. We drink our coffee together, but there's no tingle of expectation or tension of anticipation. In thirty-two years of marriage we have sipped breakfast coffee together 11,680 times. Instead of appreciating and valuing the comfort, we decide that the absence of tingle, expectation, and delightful tension means we're not happy.
It may be helpful to know that we're not supposed to be [constantly] happy. We're supposed to be comfortable. Happy is a high; it's something out of the ordinary. The norm is *comfort.* It's when we think the norm ought to be a daily high that we decide life is blah.[2]

The Joy of Sexual Freedom
This isn't to deny that we can experience considerable sexual pleasure throughout the lifetime of even a long marriage. Yes, there is romantic chemistry—sometimes intense—sparked by newness and mystery in a relationship. Yet the nature of the sexual relationship is such that its greatest pleasures can occur only in the context of trust, long-term commitment and—*familiarity.* Again, we're talking of a well-kept secret here, a very well-preserved one. It's the fact that sexual enjoyment doesn't have to diminish over the years and decades of an enduring marriage but has, in fact, great potential to increase.

For sexual joy to blossom, there must be an absence of pressure to perform, and this freedom is more likely to occur in marriage than in any other context. Marriage provides the one setting where the sexual relationship can flourish apart from guilt and regret. From the practical angle, there are critical lessons in any sexual relationship which can only be learned over time, with much patience, trial and error. From experience alone—typically *long* experience—a couple discovers how best to relate to each other physically. Many little rituals and subtle responses develop, along with a private language, which are part of a couple's treasured shared experience. Most important, within marriage alone one can be confident that the experience of sex is blessed by God. This sexual relationship can be a legitimate area of prayer, where we ask for God's help and guidance and experience his nurture and healing. Marriage also makes possible the extraordinary benefit of *thankfulness* in sex. The committed Christian couple can enjoy sex with gratitude to God—for giving them to one another, for his gift of life and health and the gift of sex itself. Add to this the fact that some have a unique sense of drawing closer to the loving Creator through the sexual relationship, and you have a spiritual dimension to sex which contributes immensely to its pleasure.

Again, this spiritual dimension is a benefit *of marriage.* And it adds a magnitude of joy to sex in marriage which can intensify over the years, particularly for those in a strong relationship who are growing spiritually as well.

I'm not ignoring the fact that in many marriages romantic love grows cold over time and sexual involvement routine or nonexistent. Yet the fact remains that for a good relationship, marriage provides far and away the best environment for romance and the physical relationship to grow. For the couple who are committed to maximizing the potential of their physical relationship, the opportunity is there for a growing bond of romantic and sexual love as time progresses.

A Proper Sense of Urgency

In considering the benefits of marriage, it is also important to respect the advantage of marrying at a time in life when we can maximize the potential God has for us personally in marriage and family life. While certain features of marriage, such as communication and sexual intimacy, may benefit from a couple's age and maturity, others—moving from city to city while careers are getting underway, or chasing two-year-olds around—are usually better suited to a couple's younger years. We who fear commitment in relationships need a greater appreciation of the benefits of marrying at an age when we are most capable of handling the responsibilities married life requires.

We will also benefit from a healthy fear of missing out on the opportunity for marriage or on certain benefits of marriage we most desire. The flip side of desiring any benefit, of course, is fearing that we'll fail to obtain it. Within proper bounds, this fear is beneficial and a vital part of the motivation that spurs us to reach any personal goal. We who fear commitment usually need a much greater measure of this healthy type of fear.

Commitment-fearful people usually take too much solace in the future. The man who fears committing to an opportunity to marry comforts himself by assuming the opportunity will present itself again. "There's no rush. I've got plenty of time to deal with my reservations and later enter marriage more confidently," he reasons. Such thinking may signify admirable patience and faith—or unhealthy avoidance. Opportunities do not present themselves forever. We who fear commitment need a greater sense of urgency to seize good opportunities that come our way.

The commitment-fearful person is disadvantaged, too, by the lack of social constraint today to marry. A generation or two ago, most people felt pressured to get married as soon as possible after high school or college. The unfortunate result was that many were too anxious to marry and jumped at the first chance. Today the pendulum has swung to the other extreme. Many simply do not feel pressured enough to find an opportunity for marriage. They have an unrealistic sense of life being infinite and the prospect for marriage ever-present.

Respecting the Biological Clock
Women who want to raise children do have a strong, natural incen-

tive to marry young. Yet women face many pressures today which conflict with their maternal instinct. The urgency many feel to prove themselves professionally even when it means delaying marriage is extreme. The feminist message that a woman should prove herself adequate without a man has its impact on many women, including some who long to be married. And the increase in education and career success enjoyed by women today leads many to be more selective in choosing a mate and thus more willing to wait indefinitely for the ideal partner. The result of these factors is that many women repress their biological instinct to marry in the early childbearing years.

Women who fear commitment are particularly prone to ignore their biological clock during their twenties and early thirties. Yet by their mid-thirties, many lament having done so. I've counseled with many in their mid- or later thirties who profoundly regret having turned down previous opportunities to marry. Now they're panicked, gripped with a sense that time is running out. In this period of awakening they realize they deeply want to marry and to do so before their childbearing years expire. They fear they've sacrificed their chance for marriage and parenthood on the altar of career. Some also worry about the increasing possibility, with increasing age, of bearing a child with birth defects.

Mixing Hope and Reality
Women face a disadvantage in the area of dating at this time, as well. Statistically, a woman's chance of marrying or being considered a serious prospect for marriage decreases significantly after age thirty-five. The problem isn't just that men are instinctively attracted to younger women (the sad fact continues), but that many men are concerned about a woman's biological potential for bearing children. The fallout is felt particularly acutely by popular women who have enjoyed an active dating life. Many feel the tables have turned on them radically in their mid-thirties. Not only are fewer men asking them out, but those who are seem far less inter-

ested in marriage. Women are often stunned by this unexpected
change of fortune. Little has changed about them outwardly or in-
wardly. Yet suddenly the world of men who had earnestly sought
their company finds them less desirable.

I've observed the plight of women in the later thirties so frequently now that I feel obliged to urge women not to ignore their
biological clock or the reality of men's attitudes in weighing an
opportunity for marriage—as politically incorrect as this message
may seem to some. I voice this concern with caution, knowing that
Satan will take a message which God intends to encourage a proper
sense of stewardship and use it to induce panic. I certainly don't
mean that a woman should become frantic about growing older and
accept an opportunity for marriage that she wouldn't otherwise consider. Yet it's just as irresponsible to ignore the biological factor. It
is one of the critical indications of God's providence in considering
an opportunity for marriage and deserves as much weight as any
other factor in making the decision.

Take the case of Cyndi. She is thirty-one and has dated Bill for
over two-and-a-half years. They have a strong, supportive relationship, and Bill is eager to marry Cyndi. Cyndi is inclined to marry
Bill as well. Yet Cyndi dated frequently throughout her twenties
and enjoyed two lengthy serious relationships. She continues to be
asked out on dates by Christian men whom she finds attractive in
the large singles group at her church. Their attention is flattering,
and Cyndi finds it hard to think of focusing her affection for a lifetime solely on Bill.

On a deeper level, though, Cyndi wants to be married, longs to
have children and devote herself to family life. I believe Cyndi is
someone who needs a wake-up call. She needs to recognize that
time *is* running out to realize her dreams. She will not be capable of
bearing children forever, and the bubble of popularity she enjoys
now is likely to burst soon. Given the many positive factors in her
relationship with Bill, the biological factor should tip the scales
and lead her to decide to marry him.

Facing the Question

My purpose in urging women to respect their biological clock is not to discourage them from pursuing career goals and pursuing them passionately. Nor am I implying that it's more Christian for a woman to be an at-home wife and mother than to have a career—or that these goals must be mutually exclusive. My concern is merely to encourage women to come to grips with what they want early enough in life to be able to achieve it. The woman who by her mid-twenties decides that she wants to marry and have children, for instance, is more likely to realize her dream than the one who doesn't reach this conclusion until her mid-thirties.

To women in their mid- or later twenties who are uncertain whether they want to be married or remain single, I offer this advice. Recognize that it's equally acceptable for a Christian to be single or married, and each lifestyle has extraordinary benefits. The critical question in finding God's will is your own preference. What is it you most want to do? Can you live a fulfilling life without sexual intercourse? Do you have warm, supportive relationships that will replace loneliness to the extent that marriage would? Either singleness or marriage is a valid choice. As a point of stewardship, though, I would urge you to try to resolve which option you prefer. Take a personal retreat, and in the solitude of prayer weigh the matter carefully before Christ. And get counsel from someone qualified to help you work through the question.

If, after making a reasonable effort, you find you're still not ready to resolve the marriage versus singleness question, then don't force the issue. It's fine to stay tentative and trust God to make the matter clear in his own way and time. Only let the decision to stay tentative be a firm choice. Too often it's a default attitude.

I offer many further guidelines in *Should I Get Married?* for deciding between marriage and singleness as a life orientation and refer you to that book for further discussion. In my most recent book, *Marry a Friend,* I also look carefully at steps Christian women and men can take to find someone suitable to marry.[3]

A Wake-Up Call for Men

If it's difficult for some young women to face the reality of their biological clock, it's much more challenging for men to accept that they too have functions that decline with age. Like women, men enjoy an optimum period when they are most capable physically and emotionally of assuming certain responsibilities of marriage and family life. Men do not have the blatant reminder of dwindling time which a woman's biological clock provides. Yet men have a biological clock of their own which they need to respect in considering marriage.

As a man grows older, the stamina needed to run with young children decreases. The energy demands of raising young children are immense and usually best handled by men in their twenties and thirties. As each year passes, too, a man is further removed from the time of his own childhood and may find it more difficult to relate to the world of a child.

Whether or not a couple decides to have children, the adjustments needed to fit each other's needs are extreme. Maturity helps the process in many ways. With age and experience we may gain greater alertness to the opposite sex's needs and a clearer awareness of our own rough edges and the changes we need to make to be a loving spouse. Yet as we age, our lifestyle and expectations also become more entrenched and we find it more difficult to be flexible. Men and women both are often most capable of making the lifestyle adjustments needed for marriage in their late twenties and early thirties.

Men should give no less attention than women to the fact of their biological clock in weighing any opportunity for marriage. Men who fear commitment should remind themselves often of the benefits that come from marrying at an age when the transitions are most natural for them to make.

Plenty of Light at the End of the Tunnel

In noting the benefits of marrying younger, I don't mean to rob older singles of their hope to marry and parent children. To the older Christian I would give a very different message, and often do. Those who long to be married yet are well into their adult years should remember that God is not bound by statistics. He has radically different timetables for each of us and at any point in life can give us the grace to make the adjustments needed for marriage or parenting. As we look around us, we find countless examples of people who have found good opportunities for marriage at unlikely times in life. At any age it is always the person who remains hopeful and socially active who is most likely to find someone suitable to marry. Older singles should pray earnestly and take the wisest steps possible to put themselves in the best position to find a partner.

At every stage in life our need is to deal with reality as we now face it—bringing to it a reasonable mix of realism, hope and faith. The fact remains that if you fear commitment, you are probably banking too much on the hope on future possibilities for relationships and failing to appreciate the value of opportunities you enjoy right now. Your hope needs to be tempered strongly with a keen appreciation of your own limitations and the brevity of life itself. A greater desire for the benefits of marrying young will help keep your caution in reasonable balance. And it will enable you to better recognize God's leading in relationships and to know when he is prompting you to take the ultimate step of faith and marry.

CHAPTER THIRTEEN

A Light Burden with Great Rewards

One Sunday morning recently I faced the question even serious Christians often wrestle with every seven days: Should I go to church? Although Sunday worship is a high priority for me, my father was hospitalized and I had promised to visit him later that morning. With other responsibilities weighing on me that day, it felt like attending church was one thing too many. *Skipping just this once won't hurt,* I reasoned.

Then I considered the impact of my example on my teenage boys. Their commitment to church life is delicate, and they don't need to see their dad waffling. I remembered, too, that the pastor would probably update the congregation on my father's condition, and I knew Dad would appreciate hearing about the report.

So off I went to church, from obligation more than motivation, shaking my head a bit at the cost of commitment.

I arrived at Fourth Presbyterian ten minutes late and had to go to the balcony for a seat. I spotted a pew that was almost empty and sat down next to the aisle. A man and woman were sitting at the other end next to the wall, but my attention was drawn to the speaker at the front and I didn't notice who they were. During a get-acquainted period a few minutes later, the usually formal Dr. Robert Norris waxed unusually relational. "The early Christians showed their affection for each other in physical ways, like embracing," he observed. "Paul even commanded them to greet each other with a 'holy kiss.' Turn and welcome those around you. If you're so inclined, give someone a hug or—if appropriate—a kiss," Norris exhorted in his Welsh brogue. High expectations for God's Frozen Chosen.

I turned and moved toward the couple at the end of the pew, to find myself staring into the face of—Jack Kemp. The gargantuan former Buffalo Bills quarterback seemed taken off guard and embarrassed by the sentimental urgings proceeding from the pulpit. He shook my hand firmly and managed a brief "How ya doin'?" But there was no kiss.

I was already glad I'd come to the service. Kemp is one of the best-known political statesmen in America, and I'll long enjoy telling this story of how I almost got kissed by him! God ministers to us in many ways through the context of worship, including comic relief.

A much more significant encounter followed, though. I turned to the pew behind me to face a woman who, while not eager to kiss anyone, was desperate for some encouragement. Knowing she was to marry in several weeks, I asked, "How are the plans going for your wedding, Melissa?"

"I'm not sure," she replied. "We've had a setback." Before she could explain, the service resumed and we had to return to our seats.

I knew that Melissa and her fiancé, Steve, both in their late thirties, had approached their decision to marry carefully, and I considered them an excellent match. When I had spoken with them several weeks earlier, they were confident about going ahead and wedding plans were firm.

After the service I asked Melissa if she would like to talk, and she welcomed the chance to unload. She explained that several days before, a close friend had urged her not to proceed with marriage. She told Melissa she had received a revelation from God that he didn't want Melissa marrying Steve. Melissa was deeply troubled over the possibility of missing God's will and wondered if she should call off the wedding.

For the next hour I talked with Melissa about her predicament. The more we interacted, the more convinced I became that Melissa shouldn't change her plans. I felt that her friend was jealous of Melissa's good opportunity to marry. Rather than face her own feelings, she gave Melissa a message about "God's will"—she spiritualized her feelings, in other words. I explained my conclusion to Melissa and urged her not to be thrown off guard by her friend's insensitive tactic. I told her also that in my study of Scripture I hadn't found any indication that God ever conveys his will to us through someone else's prophecy of guidance.

Melissa was greatly relieved by my observations and by the end of our conversation decided not to cancel her wedding. All of her other friends were in favor of her going ahead, she observed. God would certainly not expect her decision to hinge on the questionable prophecy of a friend whose motives were doubtful.

As I drove home that morning I marveled at the wonder of God's providence, in having me in the right place at exactly the right time. Besides the lift I had received from a great worship service, God had brought two memorable serendipities into my life. More than anything, I was elated to have been able to encourage someone ready to cancel her wedding. I was humbled to think that my counsel might have made the difference in her going ahead. A remarkable experience for a morning when I'd come within a hair's breadth of not attending that service.

No longer was I lamenting the burdens of commitment; I was rejoicing over the rewards.

Reaping the Benefits

A wise professor of mine once observed that we never learn any

THE YES ANXIETY

new lessons in life—we simply learn the same ones over and over. This seems especially true in the spiritual realm. The lesson of that recent Sunday morning is one whose truth I've experienced on countless occasions. Yet the pressures of life, the inertia of old habits, perhaps the influence of Satan himself, make it one too easily forgotten. It's the fact that the rewards of keeping spiritual commitments greatly outweigh any burdens involved. When we're faithful to our spiritual priorities, we give Christ an opportunity to encourage us, guide us, provide for us and use our lives to benefit others.

Throughout this book I've spoken of the benefit of a growing relationship with Christ. I've noted steps that help us draw more fully on his strength and encouragement in confronting our fears. It will help now to look more closely at how we can keep that relationship itself strong. Let's consider the commitments which most help us to keep spiritual growth alive. These commitments are at the heart of a meaningful walk with Christ. And they are steps which help us become more comfortable with the habit of commitment itself.

Private Steps of Spiritual Growth

Many Christians depend too heavily on their church life—particularly the Sunday service and sermon—for spiritual enrichment and too little on their personal effort. Spiritual growth, though, hinges on the quality of my relationship with Christ more than on any other factor. The strength of any relationship springs from time spent with the person, and this is no less true in our friendship with Christ. Our spiritual growth in all areas depends greatly on time we spend privately studying and reflecting. Others can help to stimulate the process but cannot substitute for this personal time.

We cannot enjoy the full benefits of spiritual growth, either, apart from a process of *daily* renewal. Getting our spiritual batteries recharged solely on Sunday morning is (to mix the metaphor) the spiritual equivalent of eating only one meal a week. Just as we need physical sustenance daily, we need fresh spiritual input.

The most important step we can take toward growing spiritually is to spend a regular time alone with Christ. Most of us need the benefit of this private time daily. It is particularly helpful to spend this time in early morning, to be as confident as possible of being grounded in Christ for the day ahead.

How long should our quiet time ideally be? The answer varies considerably from person to person and depends in part upon our energy level and the sheer practicality of the time we have available. We will probably need to experiment to find what length of time works best for us. Most find that a period between fifteen minutes and an hour is appropriate. Yet the regularity of this time is far more important than the length. For most people, it is better to spend fifteen minutes in devotions daily than two hours on Saturday morning.

We will need to experiment also to find what routine is best to follow and should certainly feel free to vary it from time to time. As a rule we should spend some time studying Scripture, some time praying, and some time in quiet reflection—where we give Christ an unhindered opportunity to encourage us and direct our thinking.

The benefits which come from a regular devotional time contribute immensely to meeting all of our spiritual growth needs. We gain a deeper knowledge of Scripture, greater wisdom for our decisions and stronger faith. Our intimacy with Christ grows, and his grace strengthens our moral resolve. Our personal ministry is enhanced in important ways as well. The quality of our life becomes more attractive to others and our faith more appealing. And we gain a clearer understanding of Christ's direction for our ministry.

Furthermore, the Lord himself, who longs for us to respond to his love, is pleased when we spend this time with him.

Letting Grace Motivate

In speaking of the importance of a regular quiet time, I do need to offer one caution. We can fall into a legalistic mentality regarding the time commitment involved and actually become *too* committed to a devotional practice. According to the tenets of one popular seminar, we should commit ourselves to spend a specific period in devotions each day and regard the time commitment as a *cumulative* obligation. If I miss my half-hour of quiet time on Monday, for instance, I should spend an hour on Tuesday to compensate—or an hour-and-a-half on Wednesday if I miss devotions on both Monday and Tuesday.

The fallacy behind this notion is that our devotional time is intended to gain favor with God. That is to miss the point of the quiet time entirely! We spend time alone with Christ not to satisfy some moral obligation to God but to be enriched. Christ has *already* accepted us fully and forgiven us completely. We cheapen his atonement by thinking we can gain a better standing with God through the way we approach our quiet time.

If we regard our devotional time as the spiritual equivalent of getting physical nourishment, we'll avoid this compulsive outlook. I enjoy a carton of yogurt each morning for breakfast and always receive an energy boost through this simple meal. Yet if I miss my yogurt on Monday, I don't feel compelled to eat two cartons on Tuesday, or three on Wednesday, to atone for omitted breakfasts. I do recognize that I've missed certain physical benefits when I skip breakfast. Still, I pick up the next day and move on.

This is precisely the mentality we should have toward our daily devotional time. Understanding the benefits of spending private time with Christ should motivate us to keep our commitment. Yet if we miss our quiet time on a particular day, we shouldn't imagine we have to double our effort the next day to compensate. We should merely resume our normal routine.

This same grace-centered outlook should govern all of our spiritual commitments. We should understand them as *priorities,* not as legalistic obligations.

In addition to a regular quiet time, a variety of other private efforts can help us grow spiritually. We benefit from reading enlightening Christian books and articles, from listening to stimulating recordings and programs produced by Christian teachers, and especially by making a continual effort to practice Christ's presence in our lives. Our ministry roles may also require time spent in private preparation, sharpening our gifts and getting ready for specific responsibilities. Still, our devotional time is the most important step of spiritual growth we take, for through it comes the vitality to move forward at other points.

Public Steps
Chief among the public steps we take to grow spiritually is our commitment to a local church. We may benefit also from attending an independent Bible study, fellowship or support group or from helping with the work of a social service group. College students profit greatly from faithful involvement in a campus group. And if we are to benefit fully from our association with a church, we will need to participate in activities it offers beyond the Sunday worship service.

When we are not active in a church, we limit our options for growing spiritually. Yet church commitment does not come easy for most Christians, given all the other demands on their time and the extreme freedom of choice we enjoy in America and many other nations. We have to cross three hurdles if we're to make a meaningful commitment to a church and maintain it over the long haul.

1. First, we have to overcome any assumption that church participation is optional for the Christian. "Let us not give up meeting together, as some are in the habit of doing, but let us encourage one another—and all the more as you see the Day approaching" (Heb 10:25). We must be strongly convinced we need the benefits of church involvement.

2. Second, we face the challenge of choosing a church and taking steps to become active. We need clear information about the options available, good principles of judgment for making our choice and courage to overcome any fears holding us back from joining.

3. Third, we face the challenges that invariably arise once we

pass the honeymoon stage in our association with any church. What if the preaching fails to meet our expectations? Or a conflict arises with another member? Or our own needs change in some significant way? We need a sound perspective for knowing when conditions merit our leaving the church and when they don't.

Many Christians succeed in getting beyond the first and second hurdles, then stumble at the third. They overcome their natural resistance to church commitment and make a responsible choice of one to join, yet are too quick to leave if disappointment or challenges arise. The commitment-fearful person is particularly prone to abandon ship at this time.

The greatest barrier most Christians face to good judgment in decisions about church commitment is a common misconception about the church. It's the belief that the church benefits our spiritual growth mainly through the nurture it provides for us—particularly the preaching, teaching and worship services. Many assume, too, that the church should be our *primary* source of spiritual nurture. Such expectations, though, always set us up for frustration and disappointment.

Ideals and Reality
It's axiomatic that as we sink our roots into the life of any church, our expectations of being nurtured will be disappointed at many points. No preacher, Sunday-school teacher, choir, youth program or church activity can ever live up to the high expectations we have at the outset. We're attracted to a preacher, for instance, because his approach is fresh to us and his material new and challenging. But in time we become accustomed to his style and familiar with his favorite themes. His sermons are more predictable and we less frequently receive a dramatic lift. Our experience is similar with other church programs and ministries. If familiarity does not breed contempt, it does breed concern that our needs are not being fully met.

On a more serious level, we may find that a church holds doctrinal positions or policies we disagree with yet were not aware of when we joined. Or we develop personal disagreements with others in the church. *None* of these factors, however, necessarily means it's time for us to leave. It's more likely that our expectations need to be adjusted.

The nurture we receive from a church *is* important, and we should carefully consider the quality of teaching, worship and doctrinal stance when choosing a church home. Yet any church is limited in the help it can provide us, and its support can never substitute for our own private effort. We do best to think of the church's nurture as having *maintenance value* in our spiritual pilgrimage. The church provides us encouragement, stimulation and challenge to make the effort we need to put forth on the personal level to grow in Christ.

Seeing Church Commitment Dynamically

In addition, the nurture we receive is only one of the ways Christ helps us grow through our involvement in a church. He also uses two other factors. One of these is the *challenges* we experience. When we look honestly at how cherished character traits develop, we find they result more from facing challenges than from any other experience.

Church life is one of the prime arenas where God teaches us how to love and communicate with people more effectively. While our growth in relating to people comes through many positive experiences, it comes from difficult ones as well. Through a multitude of relationships and encounters in the church we learn to accept, love and even enjoy Christians who think differently from us on doctrine and matters of church life or whose personalities make them hard for us to like. Through disagreements we learn not to run from conflict but to confront it, discuss our differences, reconcile and take the sometimes critical step of humbly asking forgiveness. Through doing the work of loving one another, we get past the irritations of personality and temperament. Church is often the setting, too, where we successfully shed our biases and learn to love those of different ethnic and cultural backgrounds.

The church itself also faces a multitude of challenges where we have the opportunity to help and grow. Each church has numerous needs related to organization, finances, the maintenance and expansion of property, and the endless planning and expediting of programs. Through lending our assistance where we can, we aid the church's ministry and hone our own character and skills as well.

God will also use imperfections in a church's preaching, teaching and worship life to break me of rigid ideas about how I must be nurtured. Through faithful attendance I find that Christ often encourages and instructs me through many means beyond the church's formal teaching and worship life. A comment someone makes in passing provides exactly the counsel I need to resolve a difficult decision. A word of encouragement from someone lifts my spirits. Or Christ may use my greater openness to him in the church environment to encourage me more directly, by clarifying my thinking in some important way or giving me motivation to take a step of faith. Any of these serendipities may occur on a Sunday morning when the worship service is less than scintillating, the sermon is unrelated to my interests and the Sunday-school lesson is on the dietary regulations of Leviticus.

It would, of course, be masochistic to choose a church *because* I dislike the preaching and worship or *because* I expect to have difficult relations with the people. Yet the fact that problems arise in these areas doesn't mean my original decision to join the church was misplaced. It's just as likely that God wants to use these difficulties to my benefit, to help me grow and to deepen my dependence on Christ.

The Privilege of Personal Ministry
God helps us grow in another major way by means of our involvement with a church, and that is through our personal ministry. For many of us this is the most fulfilling part of being active in a local

congregation. Our ministry may include taking on some responsibilities we're not motivated to assume, simply because a need exists and we're available to meet it. Again, the growth that comes through tackling such challenges can be substantial. Yet if we're tracking in the direction of our spiritual gifts, our ministry will have us doing things that we find greatly enjoyable. Depending on our gifts, these responsibilities may be logistical or administrative in nature, such as setting up chairs or working on a committee; nurture-oriented, such as teaching or counseling; inspirational, such as musical performance or worship leading.

Most Christians do not give the opportunity for personal ministry nearly enough weight in considering the benefits of church involvement. They think of nurture as the main advantage and the chance to serve as merely a nice perk. This may be an acceptable outlook for new Christians, who always need a period of putting down spiritual roots before taking on major responsibility (1 Tim 3:6; 5:22). Yet as we begin to grow in Christ, our personal ministry becomes much more central to God's purpose in our being active in a church. Mature Christians should give at least as much emphasis to the opportunity to serve as to the quality of nurture in any decision to join or leave a church. If you find yourself complaining, "This church just doesn't give me what I need!" ask yourself, "Am I giving the church what it needs from me?"

This understanding helps us see a church in terms of its potential rather than its problems. We are able to appreciate that God doesn't want us just to react to problems but to be an agent of change. If I'm dissatisfied with the teaching my church offers, for instance, it may be that I should take steps to solve the problem. Perhaps I should organize and lead a class myself. Or perhaps I should work with others to seek a solution to the church's teaching needs. Appreciating my responsibility for personal ministry helps me view my church situation much more optimistically. Indeed, my most significant growth and fulfillment may come from seeking to solve the very problems that make me want to run away.

Wise Choices and Second Thoughts

With these thoughts in mind, let me suggest some principles for selecting a church and keeping our commitment to it in right perspective over time.

If we're not currently active in a church, or are new to an area and starting from scratch, we should allow ourselves a reasonable period to "shop around." We should get the best information we can on church options and visit as many services and Sunday-school classes as possible. Two to three months is usually appropriate for this information gathering.

We should be guided in our search by high expectations but by a healthy dose of realism as well. Our goal shouldn't be to find a perfect church but the *best* alternative available where we live. We should look for the congregation offering the best mix of solid preaching, inspiring worship, instructive Sunday school, accurate doctrine, programs relevant to our family members, and traditions and policies with which we're comfortable. We should also carefully consider our prospects for having a ministry once we begin to be active in the church. Is this church open to my using my spiritual gifts, and does it need the help I can provide?

The church choices are always limited in any area, and we will invariably have to make compromises if we're to enjoy the benefits of church involvement. Here a strong conviction about God's providence helps. We should accept as a matter of faith that the church option which best meets our needs is the one God sees as right for us, even though it falls short of our ideals at some points. Remembering how we benefit from challenges and imperfections in our church experience will help us adjust our expectations to reality.

Appreciating the role of God's providence should also encourage us not to extend our church search indefinitely. We should assume that once we've made a reasonable effort to explore the options, we have exactly the information we need to choose wisely. After several months of searching at most, we should join the church which most obviously matches our needs and gifts.

From this point on we should think of our relationship to the church as a marriage of sorts. I say "of sorts" because our church commitment is not as binding as a marriage and may be broken under certain conditions. Yet the marriage analogy is appropriate, for our commitment to a church should be taken very seriously. We should be slow to conclude that any frustrations we experience are reason to leave. We should always consider carefully whether problems are simply opportunities to learn patience or are ones we should take steps to solve—even prime situations for using our gifts. In every case we should look upon challenges as prized opportunities for growth.

We should put the burden of proof strongly upon God to show us if we should discontinue our association with a church. Any decision to leave should be resolved slowly and cautiously. We should spend liberal time praying about it and wait for God to provide a clear conviction about what to do. We will do well, too, to seek the counsel of several insightful Christians who are not members of the church and are in a good position to advise us objectively.

If I instinctively fear commitment, or have a history of quitting churches after short periods of membership, I should be even more hesitant to leave. I should remember my tendency to act impulsively and make a conscious effort to counteract it. Apart from the most compelling evidence, I shouldn't conclude that God is leading me to pull up stakes and move elsewhere. I should assume that the challenges I'm facing in this church will be used by Christ to my benefit. My involvement with this church may well be a God-given opportunity to overcome my anxieties about commitment and to strengthen my ability to keep the promises I make. I should remind myself of the extraordinary benefits of staying faithful to a church even when problems arise, and I should focus on these benefits to the point that I earnestly desire them. Doing so will help me find the strength to stand firm.

CHAPTER FOURTEEN

Face Your Doubts and Do It Anyway

At age thirty-three Nancy Oliver faced the challenge of her life. All the indications were she should marry Jeff LeSourd. He was the kind of mature, compassionate, family-centered Christian man she had long prayed God would provide for her. His own family background was healthy, supportive and spiritually strong. Jeff had been magnanimously patient with Nancy and her long and winding path to resolving her feelings about marrying him.

Jeff had a solid job and would clearly be a good provider. Most important, he was a deep Christian. He loved Christ and was eager to grow spiritually. And he loved people and had many lasting friendships.

Jeff dearly loved Nancy and earnestly wanted to marry her. There was one small problem, though. Nancy wasn't romantically attracted to Jeff. The volcanic chemistry Nancy had always assumed would be present when her prince had finally come simply wasn't there.

Nancy and Jeff had come to the point of considering marriage through an unusual odyssey. Several Christian friends whom they both respected had concluded they were an ideal match. Never mind that Jeff, a resident of St. Louis, and Nancy, who lived in Virginia, had never met. Their friends urged them to communicate, and Jeff began phoning Nancy. For several months they held court—or more accurately, courtship—through long phone calls on many evenings. Their talks were blatantly honest from the beginning. These two busy professionals both knew they were taking time out of life to develop a telephone friendship for one reason: friends thought they should marry. Eventually they shared intimate details of their lives and explored the option of marriage from every angle. All of this before ever meeting face to face.

Jeff and Nancy's affection for each other grew considerably during this long-distance courtship. They concluded they should marry if they could cross one hurdle: physical chemistry. They would need to meet in person and find that they felt enough romantic attraction for each other to justify marriage.

Nancy describes that first meeting in her book *No Longer the Hero*. It took place at Washington's National Airport:

As I stared at the men walking up the ramp, I noticed one man with a huge grin on his face. He gave me a quick wave and I knew this was Jeff. . . .

"Nancy!" He exclaimed. "Finally!" He gave me a hug and we both began talking at the same time as we walked toward baggage claim.

"How was your flight?" "Did you have to wait long?" "Can I carry anything?" The words tumbled out of both of our mouths as we searched for common ground in this awkward situation. We talked for a long time as we waited for Jeff's suitcase. Finally, Jeff pierced through the formalities with one statement. "Nancy, you passed the physical test." He saw me blanch and then lower my eyes. He hurriedly added, "Let me explain what I mean by that. I meant that if I were at a party and I saw you across the room, I would be attracted enough to you to want to go over and meet you. Could you say the same about me?"

Jeff got his answer in my silence. I didn't want to hurt him, but I felt no physical attraction to him at all, even though he was nice looking. I didn't understand it. It was the most disappointing moment of my life.[1]

Surprising Advice

Bob Newman wasn't surprised to hear that Nancy wasn't physically attracted to Jeff. Nor did it deter his own conviction that Nancy should marry Jeff. He knew Nancy too well. He had counseled her for eight years, edging her over a mountain of conflicts stemming from a highly abusive childhood. Nancy, a brilliant attorney, had worked hard at the process and benefited greatly. The fact that she was even open to a relationship with someone like Jeff was a milestone.

Nancy's relationship history until now had been a field of broken dreams. She had been highly attracted to many men and pinned her hopes on dozens of relationships which either failed to develop or fizzled after a short time. Gradually Nancy grew to suspect something was fundamentally wrong with her outlook on men and romance. The relationship with Jeff forced her to confront the issue head-on.

Through Bob Newman's help and Jeff's patient encouragement, Nancy reached a conclusion as stunning as it was liberating. She realized she was incapable of being romantically attracted to the type of man who was right for her to marry. The insights in Connell Cowan and Melvyn Kinder's *Smart Women, Foolish Choices,* which Jeff gave Nancy to read, brought the problem into focus. Nancy fit the self-defeating pattern Cowan and Kinder talk about. She instinctively linked romantic love with *longing*—craving for a relationship that underneath she knew she couldn't have. Once she knew a man was available, the basis for romantic chemistry was gone.[2]

Bob Newman took the point a step further. He explained to Nancy that her capacity for feeling had been so fractured during childhood that her emotions could never be a reliable guide in any major decision. Then came her counselor's startling suggestion. She should marry Jeff even though she didn't feel in love with him. Nancy relates the conversation:

"Let's talk about feelings, Nancy. You can't go by your feelings. They have been damaged for years. Severely damaged. They are unpredictable barometers of what it is you are really thinking. In fact, often they will lie to you. You can't trust them. You shouldn't trust them."

"But certainly I can't marry Jeff without being in love with him," I protested.

"Why not?" Bob asked.

"Why not?" I repeated. "Bob, surely you wouldn't expect me to marry someone without loving them!"

"That's not what I said. You said you couldn't marry Jeff without being 'in love' with him. You were talking about your feelings about Jeff. I think it is perfectly reasonable to expect that you could marry someone without feeling you were in love."[3]

Surprised by Joy

Nancy was astounded by her counselor's advice. Yet she had to consider the source. Bob did not advise lightly or frequently, and when he did, his wisdom was impeccable. He knew her better than any soul on earth. And he earnestly desired God's best for her. Nancy agreed to give it further thought.

She finally concluded Bob was right. His explanation of how she functioned made sense; years of dating experience bore it out. If she was to realize her longstanding dream of marriage and parenthood, she would have to take control of her psyche. Apart from the outrageous step Bob suggested, her instincts would always overrule her better judgment. She would have to defy her feelings and do what her reason said was best.

And so she did.

Nancy and Jeff were married in 1986. Nancy wasn't certain if feelings of love would follow the step of marriage, and Bob made no promise that they would. Yet today she proclaims to the world that she is madly in love with Jeff. I know Jeff and Nancy personally and can attest that Nancy's testimony is not just a nice made-for-Christian-literature story. Their marriage is one of the most inspiring I have seen. Their relationship is strong, supportive and growing. They immensely enjoy sharing life together. And their example has inspired many others to move beyond their doubts and commit to marriage.

Nancy's friends were right. Bob Newman was right. Nancy herself was right—to trust her better judgment and take a monumental step of faith.

Pause for Thought
I'm not certain how Nancy's example strikes you. Perhaps you find it inspiring on one level, yet not clearly relevant to your own life. It is too extreme and atypical to be an example you would ever think of following. You cannot conceive of going into marriage without feeling in love romantically. Nor can you imagine taking any major step without strong confidence of God's leading and certainty about your own desires.

Yet, in all honesty, are you capable of reaching such a point of conviction? What does your past suggest? Do you have a history of often overlooking good opportunities in any area? Have you often walked away from prime opportunities when the chance came to commit yourself? Do you display any of the commitment-fear patterns discussed in this book—a perfectionist mentality, a dread of success, an excessive fear of losing ownership of your life? Do you find it painfully hard to resolve decisions because of persistent ambivalence or frequent mood swings?

If your answer to any of these questions is yes, I would urge you to give Nancy's example more than passing consideration. It may hold the key to breaking the cycle of indecisiveness which has held you back from God's best.

Many of us who fear commitment will be startled to realize that at one point in our life we took a step as radical and outrageous as Nancy's. And even more far-reaching. I'm speaking of our decision to commit our life to Christ. We forget just how uncertain and frightened we were about doing this. We had a myriad of unanswered questions. Our pride tugged at us powerfully and told us not to go ahead. We weren't certain if we loved Christ. We weren't at all convinced we should surrender the rest of our life into his hands. A big part of us wanted to hold back from making this commitment and keep our options open.

Yet somehow the idea of taking a step of faith took hold. Others assured us that in spite of our doubts, uncertain feelings and prideful concerns, we would be far happier living for Christ. It was time to let our better judgment take charge, they said. All of this made sense on a certain level. But even up to the moment of asking Christ into our life we wavered.

We now eagerly tell others this decision was by far the most important of our life. We recognize now what we simply couldn't with foresight—that taking this step was essential to resolving many of our doubts and fears. Only in a relationship with Christ could we appreciate many of the benefits of following him. And only by opening ourselves to his influence could we understand issues of the faith which had long puzzled us. Since giving our life to Christ we have grown remarkably, and our love for him has deepened greatly.

It's plain to us now that we couldn't have become a Christian apart from a significant psychological transformation. Before giving our life to Christ we were incapable of understanding what a relationship with him was like. Remembering how mistaken our impressions of it were helps us realize how capable we are of missing what is in our best interest. It becomes easier to appreciate that our feelings can deceive us in decisions today as well.

Revising the Map
We imagine that conversion is an experience we need to go through

only one time. But while we need to give our life to Christ just once, our blind spots in other areas don't begin to clear up immediately. Understanding God's best for our life is a continuing challenge, requiring many adjustments in our expectations. This is Paul's point when he urges, "Be transformed by the renewing of your mind" (Rom 12:2). The Greek verb for *be transformed* is in a tense that indicates ongoing action. Paul is exhorting us to constantly make the effort to reshape our outlook into one which reflects God's intentions for us. From this standpoint, conversion is a *lifetime* process.

What does this imply, then, for our major decisions and commitments? Will finding God's best in marriage or career, for instance, require a transformation as extreme as what I went through in accepting Christ? Possibly. Possibly not. It all depends on why I resist commitment and how deeply entrenched my inhibitions are.

Nancy LeSourd illustrates one extreme. Her childhood background was so abusive and dysfunctional that it severely injured her ability to make reliable emotional judgments. Hers was not merely a problem of mood swings—feeling in love with Jeff one day but uncertain the next, for example. She was *incapable* of feeling attracted to a man who would be right for her. For her, finding God's best required an extraordinarily courageous step—going forward with marriage because all the other indications were there even though her feelings weren't.

Some of us who are uncomfortable with commitment may be coming from a very different place. Our family background was relatively healthy. The prospect of commitment doesn't arouse panic or severe anxiety. Still, we find it hard to resolve certain decisions. We may be hindered by unrealistic ideals or expectations of God giving us perfect peace. Simply finding that God's best can seem less than perfect, that it's okay to make tradeoffs, and that absolute certainty of God's will isn't required may be enough to get us over the hump. While we may feel nervous finally resolving a commitment, we don't feel as though we're living on the edge.

Many of us who fear commitment are somewhere between these two points. While our family background wasn't outright abusive, it was far less supportive than we wished. We're not incapable of feeling attracted to options that are right for us. Yet our feelings aren't consistent, and mood swings are a serious problem. The thought of resolving a decision and locking into one choice once and for all arouses more than mild anxiety.

For us, the critical need is to examine our pattern of feelings over time and give the weight to what we think during our periods of best judgment. The point comes when we need to take a bold step to break our cycle of fluctuating emotions. We need to side with our best judgment and commit ourselves in light of what it tells us—even though our impressions continue to vacillate. Committing ourselves at this time may seem no less risky, no less extreme than the step of faith we took to commit our life to Christ. It may for all the world feel like we're going through another conversion experience. Yet it will be essential to take hold of God's best in the areas where commitment frightens us.

Taking the Challenge

The two greatest challenges we face in making commitments are these:
- *To know ourselves.*
- *To take control of what we know.*

On the one hand, we need to carefully consider why we resist commitment and what it is we fear. We need to recognize the factors in our backgrounds which make us prone to fear commitment. And we need to clarify the concerns we have about committing ourselves.

With this self-understanding in mind, we need to make a strategic effort to counteract the tendencies which keep us from committing to good opportunities. Throughout this book I've suggested changes in outlook and practical steps which can help us do that.

No matter how conscientiously we follow these steps, though, the point still comes where we need to go ahead with commitments even though our emotions vacillate and "all the facts are not in." Again, I realize what I'm advising flies in the face of much advice offered by respected teachers in the body of Christ today. In the most popular Christian book currently available on finding a marriage partner, the author sounds a consistent theme: When in doubt, don't. Do not proceed with marriage if you have any reservations whatever. At one point he even cautions, "Don't be afraid to walk away from the relationship at *any* time *before* you say your vows— even if it is while you are standing before a minister, priest or rabbi!"[4]

While this advice may have value for Christians in their teens and young twenties who need some proper caution against jumping into marriage too quickly—even at the expense of hyperbole— it wreaks havoc for older singles who instinctively fear committing to marriage. They are psychologically unable to reach such a point of sublime conviction; many are not able to come anywhere close. *Ever.* Only by taking a courageous step of faith can these people break the bind of their fears and move forward with a good opportunity for marriage.

It will take an equally courageous step for many of us to settle into the best opportunities God has for us in career, spiritual life and other areas. By going ahead with commitment in spite of hesitations, we best position ourselves to enjoy two unsurpassable benefits. One is the transformation that occurs within us: we instinctively look for ways to maximize our fulfillment and effectiveness in situations to which we're committed. And the other: through commitment we open ourselves to the fullest blessings of God, who in countless ways rewards those who take calculated steps of faith.

The Joy of Commitment

I don't know what decisions you are facing or what your personal hesitations are about commitment. I am certain of several things, though. You will find over the course of your life that the richest provision of Christ for your needs occurs within the context of commitments you make. Your greatest experiences of joy will take place within these commitments as well. These commitments will include many that are difficult to make and some that you enter with fear and trembling. Learning to say yes and mean it is the most important step you can take toward experiencing the abundant life Christ spoke so fervently about. It is also the most critical step toward realizing your potential. God has certain goals for us each to accomplish during our life, in career, relationships and personal ministry. We constantly need the reminder—gentle and not so gentle—that our time on earth isn't infinite. While God gives us treasured opportunities in each of these areas, he does not extend them to us forever. Finding his best requires zeal, and it requires decisiveness. It means choosing among options, resolving decisions—forging commitments. It was in this spirit that Paul urged Timothy, in each of his letters to him, to "rekindle the gift" and "not neglect the gift" God had given him (2 Tim 1:6 RSV; 1 Tim 4:14 RSV).

I sincerely hope you have found this book helpful in your pilgrimage with commitment. I trust that its insights, and especially the biblical material, have helped you grow more comfortable with making commitments. As you move forward, I would urge you to keep in mind Christ's unending commitment to love you, protect you, guide you and provide you with the best possible opportunities for investing your life. Take heart that you serve the One in whom all the promises of God are yes (2 Cor 1:20).

Be encouraged by his example as well. Jesus, God the Son, came into earthly life aware of endless needs throughout the world that deserved his attention. He could have gone anywhere in the world to minister and made a drastic difference. Yet he chose to concentrate for just three years in a small segment of the populated earth and never traveled more than a hundred miles from his home. He spent much of this time discipling just twelve men. He focused. He committed himself. And he changed the course of history forever.

May his example encourage you as you make tough choices within the maze of options in your own life. And may it inspire you to make commitments with greater confidence.

Notes

Chapter Two: Seeing the Best When it's Less Than Perfect
[1]Connell Cowan and Melvyn Kinder, *Smart Women, Foolish Choices* (New York: Clarkson N. Potter/Crown, 1985), p. 63.

Chapter Three: Tradeoffs Worth Making
[1]Quoted in Ellen Goodman, *Turning Points* (New York: Fawcett Crest, 1979), p. 30.

[2]Peter G. Hanson, *The Joy of Stress* (Kansas City: Andrews, McMeel and Parker, 1985), pp. 45-46, 72-73, 104-5.

[3]André Bustanoby, *Can Men and Women Be Just Friends?* (Grand Rapids, Mich.: Pyranee, 1985), pp. 116-19.

[4]Paul Tournier, *The Adventure of Living* (New York: Harper & Row, 1965).

Chapter Four: Facing Our Fears of Success
[1]Martha Friedman, *Overcoming the Fear of Success* (New York: Warner, 1980), pp. 159-68.

[2]Judith S. Wallerstein and Sandra Blakeslee, *Second Chances: Men, Women and Children a Decade after Divorce* (New York: Ticknor

and Fields, 1990), p. 101.
[3]Tournier, *The Adventure of Living,* pp. 97-98.

Chapter Five: Overcoming Our Fears of Success
[1]Ibid., p. 113.
[2]Friedman, *Overcoming the Fear of Success,* p. 191.
[3]Ibid.

Chapter Six: Owning Your Life
[1]Paul Tournier, *The Person Reborn* (New York: Harper & Row, 1966), pp. 139-73.

Chapter Seven: Breaking the Grip of Mood Swings
[1]An increase in estrogen during the first half of the cycle enhances alertness and well-being. Progesterone rises during the second half of the cycle, decreasing energy and libido but also having a tranquilizing effect. Levels of both hormones plummet four or five days prior to menstruation. The loss of both the energizing effect of estrogen and the calming influence of progesterone leaves some women feeling jittery or depressed.
[2]The loss of testosterone following sexual intimacy leads to an emotional letdown for most men. The effect is typically lessened energy, loss of sexual and romantic interest and decreased zeal in other areas. While some women experience a similar letdown following sexual relations, the emotional drop is usually not as sharp as the male's.

Chapter Eight: Guidance and Intuition
[1]See my *Knowing God's Will: Finding Guidance for Personal Decisions* (Downers Grove, Ill.: InterVarsity Press, 1991), pp. 166-67 and footnote 1 on p. 167.
[2]Nita Tucker with Debra Feinstein, *Beyond Cinderella: How to Find and Marry the Man You Want* (New York: St. Martin's Press, 1987), p. *57.*

Chapter Nine: When Fear Takes on a Life of Its Own

[1]M. Blaine Smith, *Overcoming Shyness* (Downers Grove, Ill.: InterVarsity Press, 1993), pp. 73-75, 78-79.

Chapter Eleven: The Best-Kept Secret of Career Success

[1]Carole Hyatt and Linda Gottlieb, *When Smart People Fail* (New York: Penguin, 1987), pp. 103-4.

Chapter Twelve: Going for the Gold in Relationships

[1]Bustanoby, *Can Men and Women Be Just Friends?* p. 118.
[2]Ibid., pp. 118-19.
[3]M. Blaine Smith, *Should I Get Married?* (Downers Grove, Ill.: InterVarsity Press, 1990); M. Blaine Smith *Marry a Friend: Finding Someone to Marry Who Is Truly Right for You* (Damascus, Md.: SilverCrest Books, 2011).

Chapter Fourteen: Face Your Doubts and Do It Anyway

[1]Nancy LeSourd, *No Longer the Hero: The Personal Pilgrimage of an Adult Child* (Nashville: Thomas Nelson, 1991), pp. 246-47.
[2]See pp. 21-22 of *The Yes Anxiety* for further discussion of Cowan and Kinder's book.
[3]LeSourd, *op. cit.,* p. 259.
[4]Neil Clark Warren, *Finding the Love of Your Life* (Colorado Springs, Colo.: Focus on the Family, 1992), p. 136, italics Warren's.

About the Author

Blaine Smith, a Presbyterian pastor, spent 30 years as director of Nehemiah Ministries, Inc., a resource ministry based in the Washington, D.C. area. He retired the organization in 2009, but continues to use the name Nehemiah Ministries for free-lance work.

His career has included giving seminars and lectures, speaking at conferences, counseling, and writing. He is author of nine books, including *Knowing God's Will* (original and revised editions), *Should I Get Married?* (original and revised editions), *The Yes Anxiety*, *Overcoming Shyness*, *The Optimism Factor*, *One of a Kind*, and *Marry a Friend*, as well as numerous articles (all books except *Marry a Friend* published by InterVarsity Press). These books have been published in more than thirty English language and international editions. He is also lecturer for *Guidance By The Book*, a home study course with audio cassettes produced by the Christian Broadcasting Network as part of their *Living By The Book* series.

Blaine served previously as founder/director of the Sons of Thunder, believed by many to be America's first active Christian rock band, and as assistant pastor of Memorial Presbyterian Church in St. Louis. He is an avid guitarist, and currently performs with the

Newports, an oldies band active in the Washington, D.C. area. Blaine is a graduate of Georgetown University, and also holds a Master of Divinity from Wesley Theological Seminary and a Doctor of Ministry from Fuller Theological Seminary. He and Evie live in Gaithersburg, Maryland. They've been married since 1973, and have two grown sons, Benjamin and Nathan. Their first grandchild, Jackson Olen, was born to Ben and his wife Lorinda in 2009.

Blaine also authors a twice-monthly online newsletter, *Nehemiah Notes*, featuring a practical article on the Christian faith, posted on his ministry website and available by e-mail for free. You may e-mail Blaine at mbs@nehemiahministries.com.

Made in the USA
San Bernardino, CA
05 March 2014